Extraordinary Tales
from Manitoba History

J. W. Chafe

Illustrated by Peter Kuch

Published under the auspices of the Manitoba Historical
Society in association with McClelland and Stewart Limited

ISBN 0-7710-1951-3

The Canadian Publishers
McClelland and Stewart Limited
25 Hollinger Road, Toronto.

The Manitoba Historical Society wishes to acknowledge the Manitoba Centennial Corporation, Government of Manitoba, for assistance received in the form of a grant.

The views expressed by the author are not necessarily those of the Society.

PRINTED AND BOUND IN CANADA

Acknowledgements

The men and women who "were there" and created or told the stories – while they were still "hot" – were the people who wrote this book. I simply gathered their accounts together, tried to warm them up, and put them between covers. I could not have done that, of course, without the work of many dozens of historians who so ably recorded the stories in books down through the years.

I am grateful, too, to the Manitoba Historical Society for sponsoring the book; and especially to its dedicated Past President, W. Steward Martin, who master-minded this and other projects.

History-conscious Manitobans like Jim Jackson and Ed Russenholt, who read the manuscript, don't ask to be thanked; they just want to help add a dimension to the lives of others by sharing, vicariously, in the adventures of earlier Manitobans.

J. W. CHAFE

Contents

Preface

This Book is about People. Only in old-fashioned textbooks is the province of Manitoba depicted as a slab of the earth's crust upon which certain events have occurred. Manitobans have done things – unusual, tragic, funny things – which, if not historically important, are nevertheless interesting. And they are all certainly an integral part of our heritage.

"Manitobans," of course, means not just the Anglo-Saxons or the French, but all who, since 1870, have made their homes here. And we Manitobans of the 1970's can be proud that we recognize this simple fact. Almost from the creation of the province the Anglo-Saxons have been the dominant group; and living on an English-speaking continent, for decades they regarded themselves as the "real" Manitobans. Their children and grandchildren today are above such arrogance.

The children and grandchildren of the immigrants from Europe can also be proud. They have proven themselves worthy of the sacrifices made for them by their parents; they have earned the respect of the dominant group; and they have risen above the resentments early immigrants quite justifiably felt.

This does not mean they have become imitation Anglo-Saxons – that they are ashamed of their origins, that they have betrayed their cultural inheritance. On the contrary, they are proud of their parents' language. On New Year's Day, 1972, the *Free Press* greeted its readers in 118 languages; which means that people in all walks of life are keeping alive their mother tongues.

So our province has that precious ingredient – richness in diversity. On Main Street in Winnipeg an Anglican cathedral stands near an onion-domed Greek Orthodox church and a twin-turreted Ukrainian Catholic church. Gifted sons and daughters of Manitobans born in Europe or elsewhere enrich our Ballet, Symphony Orchestra, Theatre Centre, and Musical Festival. No doubt most citizens are grateful for the colour this adds to life on the prairies.

What is this part of the earth's surface we occupy like? If we think of it as slanting – running gradually downhill – from south, east and west, towards Hudson Bay, we have the essential feature. And this fact basically determined our early history, simply because water runs downhill. As for the nature of the surface, it is chiefly prairie in the south, large lakes in the middle, with rock, muskeg, rivers, and many more lakes in the north. The number of lakes is unbelievable: something like 100,000. Many of these, it is said, have yet to be seen by a white man.

It will probably be another century before we discover what a treasure house our Northland is, although the progress we have already made has been impressive. The head of the International Nickel Company in Italy visited Thompson's mining and refining complex recently and his comment was: "Extraordinary – absolutely unique!" The North is also an unspoiled – and unpolluted – summer and winter playground. In fact, some of it has been taken over by Americans who recognize that it is an easily accessible part of the "last, best North."

Americans seem to like Canada, and one of the chief reasons they give is that there is "less violence" here. It's true of course. Moreover, we have no tradition of violence; we have tried to solve our problems by compromise, not by shooting at each other. But we have, in a sense, paid a price for this. Compromise is not exciting – shooting is. So today's Canadians in general know little of their history, and read little of it because it is considered "dull." In fact, it is even doubtful if Canadian children respond to the deeds of our "fighting" heroes, men like Radisson and d'Iberville, as much as to the exploits of the Kit Carsons and the Wyatt Earps.

But Manitoba's past, like Canada's, is far from dull; it is chockfull of hair-raising episodes and "believe-it-or-not" happenings. There were thousands of buffalo hunters who could load and shoot with amazing speed and accuracy from the saddle at a gallop. There was no Jesse James, but there was a fascinating confidence man who had practised on wealthy Americans. No John Paul Jones, but a French-Canadian sea captain who, just off York Factory, fought three British men-of-war with his one ship and made monkeys of them. No Davy Crockett, but a lad who sucessfully took on two grizzlies. No "Defenders of the Alamo," but a little band of Métis who won a victory over a horde of Sioux warriors as brilliant as anything in Homer. No George Washington, but a Scot at Portage la Prairie who made himself President of a brief "Republic of Manitobah." No world-champion cyclist, but an early Manitoba highwheel champion who returned to ride in Winnipeg's 1949 anniversary parade – at the age of ninety-one. And then there was the ex-circus clown who used to dress up as a minister of the Gospel, go out on the street, mince up to a group of greenhorns from the east, and swear like a mule driver, just to see their faces!

Believe it or not, all this – and much more – happened in Manitoba.

CHAPTER 1

Battle for Beaver: British vs. French (1670-1763)

It All Started Three Hundred Years Ago. The year 1970 was Manitoba's hundredth anniversary; but, in a sense, it was more than the three hundredth. White people of various origins have been visiting or living here since before 1668, when the British began trading for furs.

Actually, sixty years before the Hudson's Bay Company was officially started in 1670, one white man traded with one Indian in the North (although Vikings may have beaten even him by nearly six hundred years). The man was Henry Hudson, and he hadn't set out to get furs; he was searching for the North-West Passage. A short route to the Orient had become the Holy Grail to explorers, and Hudson is recognized as the first to get through the ice-infested strait into the inland sea, both of which were to be named after him. His ship was trapped on the east coast of James Bay by the ice, so he and his crew had the dubious distinction of being the first recorded whites to spend a winter in the Canadian North.

In the spring they had a visitor. One day a lone Indian, with a roll of furs on his back, approached their camp timidly. His eyes saucered at the sight of the wonder-tools and trinkets these white-faced creatures from another world showed by signs they were willing to give him – just for animal skins! He gleefully handed over the skins of two deer and two beaver for a knife, a hatchet, some beads, and a little mirror.

But the east coast of James Bay is Quebec territory. The first recorded white man to set foot on Manitoba soil was Thomas Button in 1612. (Six families living in Winnipeg claim descent from him.) In two ships, the *Resolution* and the *Discovery,* But-

11

ton's party crossed Hudson Bay, searched for an outlet westward that would take them to the far East, discovered the mouth of the Nelson River, and then, like Hudson, was trapped by winter. Landfall at this location was to prove important. Fort York (York Factory), which the HBC established in the vicinity later, became the key link in the fur-trade chain stretching between the interior, where the furs were found, and London, where they were turned into gold.

The explorer who followed Button, Danish sea captain Jens Munck, discovered the mouth of the Churchill River (so named, later, after an illustrious ancestor of Winston Churchill). Munck's Protestant chaplain, Rev. Rasmus Jensen, became the first to conduct a religious service in Western Canada; and Munck and his men were the first to *eat grass,* or rather he and two of his men were. All the others (sixty-two of them) died of scurvy before the end of the winter. Either they hadn't heard of the Indian remedy, the juice of boiled spruce needles, or they couldn't find any spruce trees. The three survivors wouldn't have given a *krone* for their own chances, till one of them after break-up tried eating sorrel grass. It cured them and somehow they managed to sail one of their two ships back to Denmark.

Two Frenchmen Start an English Fur Company. In the early 1660's, New France's adventurous fur traders, Radisson and Groseilliers, found themselves on the great watershed from which the rivers flowed either to Lake Superior or to what the Crees called "The Sea of the North." They also heard Indian tales of a large body of water to the west called the Stinking Lake, probably Lake Winnipeg; and that it too emptied into the northern sea. They came to the conclusion that "The Sea of the North" and Hudson Bay were one and the same. If so, they reasoned, the best way to reach the best fur country – generally, the farther north the better the furs – was not by the long and difficult St. Lawrence-Great Lakes route but by Hudson Bay; besides the possibility that perhaps the Bay was closer to France than was Montreal. (They were right in both respects.)

They could hardly wait to return to Quebec with their furs and their great idea. When they did, the Governor of New France, instead of hailing them as empire-builders, seized more than two-thirds of their furs – on the pretext that they hadn't asked his permission to trade.

12

Radisson and Groseilliers were outraged. Declaring that if they were going to be mistreated in New France they would try New England, they set out for Boston. And there a chance meeting with a government official from England changed the course of North American history. The official suggested that they accompany him to England and tell their story to the Court. They did just that, gaining the ear of Charles II, the "Merry Monarch" – the leading playboy in the Nell Gwyn crowd.

Charles was clearly interested; the Frenchmen's scheme might well give England a dominant position in the fur trade, and for a special reason. Fur, which meant primarily beaver, was a luxury item; it was *de rigueur* for every gentleman in Europe to wear a beaver hat. And from the northern regions, as Radisson pointed out, came the kind of beaver that was best for felting; it provided the best *wool* for making hats.

Charles's cousin, the dashing Prince Rupert, was interested too and he organized a group willing to risk money on a trading venture to Hudson Bay. They persuaded the King that a trial run should be made, and in June of 1668 two ships set sail: the *Nonsuch,* captained by Zachary Gillam, with Groseilliers aboard, and the *Eaglet,* with Radisson. The *Eaglet* sprang a leak and had to go back, but the *Nonsuch* got through. Groseilliers knew how to get furs and the next summer there was great excitement in England. The *Nonsuch* had returned with a valuable cargo of furs.

But Prince Rupert and his associates were worried that others might horn in on their bonanza, so they appealed to the King. He gave them a monopoly. On May 2, 1670, he signed the famous charter – it was seven thousand words long – giving "the Governor and Company of Adventurers of England Trading into Hudson's Bay" sole right to the fur trade in all the lands draining into the Bay, as well as the right to rule those lands with everything and everybody therein. The "Adventurers" were to be "true and absolute Lordes and Proprietors," which meant they would have more power in their domain than Charles himself had in England. Their territory, although the King had no way of knowing it, was as large as Europe.

There was one curious provision in the charter. The "Adventurers" were to turn over some of their furs to the Crown – but, as it turned out, not very often. Only "whenever Wee . . . enter into the said Countryes." And the number of furs? The skins of

13

"two Elkes and two Black Beavers." This symbolic payment has been made three times in Winnipeg: in 1927 to the Prince of Wales, in 1939 to King George VI, and in 1970 to Queen Elizabeth II.

"Radishes" and "Gooseberry" "Defect" to the French. The two free-wheeling Frenchmen had seen their great idea realized, but they weren't very happy. The Company they had helped found was only paying them wages while other men were building fortunes. And civilization with its constraints bored them. In the wilds they had been lords of all they had surveyed: "We were Caesars," wrote Radisson, "being nobody to contradict us." They craved adventure; on which side, French or English, they apparently didn't care. So when a new, aggressive Governor in New France offered them not only forgiveness but scope for their talents, they deserted, and became French again.

In 1682, they appeared on the Bay with a small party in two French ships. And what happened was pure comic opera. They knew they were more likely to avoid detection on the Hayes River than on the Nelson – the mouths of the two were separated only by a narrow tongue of land – so, under cover of darkness, they sailed ten miles up the Hayes and built a fort. One day, when Radisson was twenty miles up the Nelson, he heard gunfire and discovered, on an island, another fort, with a ship anchored beside it. Clearly this was not an HBC party.

His long years of outwitting the Iroquois had made him a master spy, and he soon ferreted out the facts. These were New Englanders! They were poachers (like his own French party) and were led by Ben Gillam, Zachary Gillam's son! As if this didn't make the plot intriguing enough, the ship was manned by bachelors only – fourteen of them! (The mate's name was John Outlaw.) Apparently they had embarked on the voyage partly as a lark. They had even renamed the ship – it was now the *Bachelor's Delight*. And their island-home had been christened "Bachelor's Island."

But the situation wasn't especially intriguing to Radisson – he had to do something about it. His partner agreed that maybe the best strategy would be to give the enemy a false sense of security. So Radisson visited Ben; and in a jovial "we're both against the HBC monopoly" manner he said that although he had a very strong force at his post (which he didn't) he would let the New

14

Englanders stay all winter – there were enough furs for all! And his men would even protect them from the dangerous Indians (they weren't dangerous, they just wanted to trade). Ben swallowed the story, and the French gleefully went on with the business of corralling most of the furs.

But one day – a second jolt: an HBC ship appeared at the mouth of the Nelson. Most people would have cut and run, but not Radisson. He boldly went aboard, as nonchalantly as if he were still with the English, and he wasn't taken prisoner. But what he found out should have made his head spin. Not only was the vessel carrying the resident Governor, Bridgar, but it was captained by Zachary Gillam, Ben's father! What to do? One thing for sure: he'd have to bluff the English too. And looking Bridgar in the eye, he declared that he had taken possession of the country in the name of the King of France, and that he had over three hundred men under his command. He actually forbade the English to go ashore. And the bluff worked.

But Radisson and Groseilliers knew that, long before spring, the two parties would discover each other, and that both being English they would probably join forces against the French. Radisson's agile brain went to work. Ah! He'd let Zachary know that his son was there, poaching. Then the elder Gillam would do all in his power to keep Bridgar from finding out. So he persuaded Ben to put on an Indian disguise and accompany him on a visit to his father. Zachary, of course, was shocked. Radisson was delighted. Again his men could get on, at least temporarily, with their poaching.

But summer was a long way off, and any one of a number of things could upset the delicate balance. After two or three bad scares, Radisson decided that if he and his partner were going to sail for Quebec with the furs gathered by all three parties, he would have to take drastic action and put both enemy parties in his power. He had "divided"; now he would "conquer."

Against the New Englanders he used the ancient "Trojan horse" trick. By means of a ruse he got two of his men inside Ben's fort, and sure enough they succeeded in opening the gates just at the crucial moment. He didn't have to attack the "old" Englanders, partly because almost every misfortune imaginable had struck them; in fact, Radisson – strange character – had been giving them food and supplies. Zachary had been able to keep Bridgar from finding out that the New Englanders were

15

there, till one of Ben's men escaped and told him. Then he naively stalked into the French fort to declare the "incontestability of the English claim," and ended up, with all his men, as Radisson's prisoner.

That summer the French did sail away with all the furs; and in the best ship, the bachelors' *Bachelor's Delight*. Aboard were Bridgar himself and the New England prisoners. Radisson let Zachary Gillam and the English crewmen sail one of the HBC ships to the company's Rupert House on James Bay. Fully intending to be back on the Bay the next year, he left a few men in the fort under Groseillier's son, Jean Baptiste. So, for a second time, the two famous French traders landed triumphantly at Quebec with a fortune in furs.

And for a second time they ran into trouble: another Governor of the wrong sort. He too seized their furs, only this time it was for *attacking the English;* the two nations were "waging peace," taking a breather between wars. To Groseilliers, who was now sixty-five years old (he was seventeen years older than his partner), such treatment was too much. He quit the fur trade and took up farming. The French Governor should have known what Radisson would do. He went back to the English and his English wife, both receiving him with open arms.

But the comic opera hadn't been quite played out. The next spring, this quick-change artist turned up on the Bay with an HBC party, looked his nephew, Jean Baptiste, in the eye, and ordered him to surrender the fort. No doubt the young fellow would have enjoyed shooting his uncle. Perhaps he saw the humour of it all; perhaps he too was "practical." In any case, he went back to England with his uncle. Great quantities of furs went back too; in fact, in 1684, the Company declared a dividend of fifty per cent.

Then Pierre Esprit Radisson, prince of rogues and heroes, just faded away. He had done much for his adopted country, although he had adopted it only because it gave him scope for his explosive talents. For himself, despite the fact that he never won the fortune he is assumed to have dreamed of, he did win honours: King Charles presented him with a "Medall and Chaine" (which he pawned when things went badly for him), and he wooed and won three English wives, one of them a daughter of the nobility. At the end of his services he was grant-

ed a good pension – which he spent, as was to be expected, with abandon – and died in poverty. But surely content.

D'Iberville Wins the Bay for the French – Temporarily. In September of 1697, two strong fleets, English and French, raced for the Bay and reached Hudson Strait at the same time. Both got locked in the ice, each within sight of the other. The first ship to break loose was the *Pelican,* the flagship of the French commander, Pierre le Moyne, Sieur d'Iberville (the most famous of twelve famous fighting French-Canadian brothers). He called for every inch of canvas she could carry and made for his target, the English post of Fort Nelson (York Factory), hoping that at least one of his other ships would break free before any of the enemy vessels did. With their combined fire-power, they could blast the fort into surrender. He reached Fort Nelson and waited. But days passed and no ships appeared. Then a sail – and another – and another ! Three of his ships were free! A cheer from the crew and the *Pelican* dashed off to meet them. Then, with the distance closing fast, a shock – they were *English* ships! D'Iberville was trapped between English guns on land and sea. But he would fight; he had no choice. David would tackle Goliath.

The largest of the three English vessels, the *Hampshire,* was the *Pelican*'s size, and d'Iberville shot straight at her. She took evasive action, while her supporting ships, the *Dering* and the *Royal Hudson's Bay* raked the *Pelican*. D'Iberville put about and attacked again, though his ship by now was a shambles, and half his crew were wounded or dead. But on she came, her guns blazing, blasting holes in the *Hampshire*'s hull. Then a miracle, or so it seemed: the English ship began to list, to founder – and sank! D'Iberville's half-crew somehow got their mangled vessel round to face the other enemy ships and – how they must have cheered – saw the *Dering* escaping! *The Royal Hudson's Bay* was striking her colours!

Then tragedy: a storm blew the two remaining ships onto shore and wrecked them both. Wounded sailors died in the icy waters, and the survivors, English and French, lay on the shore like dead men. Hours went by, when suddenly other sails appeared. This time they were French ships. Within a short time the wounded were being cared for in Fort Nelson which was now French!

Little Giant and the Grizzly Bears. From the time of the charter the English were apparently satisfied with the number of Indians bringing their furs to the Bay; they sent only one man into the interior to persuade the more distant tribes to join the parade. His name was Henry Kelsey, and when he first set out he was only nineteen years old. He had been a London street urchin with little or no education, until he was shipped out to the Bay. But he must have had great understanding and tact or he would never have come back alive.

In his journal (much of it was written in rhyme) Kelsey writes that in 1689 he was put ashore "to ye northward of Churchill river" with an Indian boy "in order to bring to a commerce ye Northern Indians." The two walked two hundred miles but saw no Indians. But they did see the "buffilo," which meant that Kelsey was probably the first white man to see, not buffalo, but muskox. They would have gone farther, but the native boy, whom Henry had named Tom Savage, was afraid of running into Eskimos, "and called me a fool because I was not conscious of the danger."

The next year, Governor Geyer, having received orders from London to send this exceptional young fellow into the regions far to the south, dispatched him with Tom Savage (and his bow and arrows) "into the country of the Assinae Poets with the Captain of that Nation." Henry Kelsey notes that:

> The inland country of good report hath been
> By Indians, but by English yet not seen.

But he saw much of it.

He was the first white man to reach the Saskatchewan River (near The Pas) and the first on the prairies. There he saw real "buffilo" (he noted the difference), watched a buffalo hunt and admired the Indians' skill; they had no horses or fire-arms, only bows and arrows.

Kelsey was probably also the first white man to see the grizzly bear, which he described later as "bigger than any white bear and neither black or white but silver haird like our English rabbit." There is no doubt of the accuracy of his description because he had a close-up look. He and Tom were travelling in the woods when suddenly they found themselves facing two of the huge creatures, a mother and her full-grown cub. Tom climbed a spruce tree, fast, and Henry leaped behind a clump of willows, priming his musket "in flight." The cub made for the tree and was trying to climb it when Henry fired and the cub dropped

19

over dead. But the mother had already started for Henry; so Tom shinnied down the tree, stood on the cub's body, and war-whooped to attract her attention. But she kept on coming, straight for Henry! Kelsey fired – but still she kept on coming! He leaped to one side, the bear roared straight on, crashed into the willows – and fell dead! It was *then* that he noted that grizzly bears are "silver haird like our English rabbit."

The news of the miracle performed by this pale-faced young man from another world, with a fire-belching, death-dealing weapon, spread far and wide, and Henry became famous as "Little Giant." He was looked on with awe, so much so that he was able to make peace between tribes on the warpath. But he proved to be quite human: he returned with an Indian wife. His marriage was not approved of by the Governor who objected to "Mistress Kelsey entering into the court." But Henry said, in effect, "Love me, love my wife," and won.

La Vérendrye Opens the Way to the West. The leader of the French traders, the first recorded white man in what is now the more populated part of Manitoba, was Pierre Gaultier de Varennes, Sieur de la Vérendrye. His purpose was not, primarily, to extend the Montreal fur trade but to find a route to the western Sea. From the start the fates seemed against him. Instead of depending solely on fur sales La Vérendrye tried to persuade the French government to bear at least some of the costs of the expensive undertaking. As it awarded him only a trading monopoly in the new lands he might reach, he had to find the capital himself. After exhausting his private resources, with great difficulty he later managed to secure backers among the merchants of Montreal. But these men were interested only in profits; and throughout his thirteen long years in the West debt was a mill-stone about his neck.

Even for a younger man in robust health such a mental strain would have been hard to bear. When La Vérendrye started out, he was forty-eight years old, had fought in Europe, suffered nine wounds, and had been left for dead on the battlefield. Oddly enough he was to find that his wounds were to be of some help in his venture. One of his crucial problems was to keep competing tribes under control; and knowing that the natives respected and admired a warrior, he sometimes awed their chiefs by showing them his old scars.

In the flotilla of canoes that left Montreal in 1731 were his three sons, Jean-Baptiste, Pierre, and François, his nephew, La Jemeraye, and a large number of *voyageurs* and soldiers. They reached the Lake of the Woods and built Fort St. Charles; and from there Jean-Baptiste and La Jemeraye pushed on to Lake Winnipeg, discovered the mouth of a river, which they named the Red, and on it built Fort Maurepas. They were, as far as is known, the first white men to see the largest of the province's big lakes.

Unexpectedly, La Vérendrye's nephew, La Jemeraye, who shared his dream, died – probably from over-exertion and exposure. And a greater tragedy followed. His eldest son, Jean-Baptiste, Father Aulneau (the expedition's chaplain), and twenty-two of his men were murdered by the Sioux on an island in the Lake of the Woods. (In the early 1900's, through the research of Judge Prudhomme and the St. Boniface Historical Society, what was believed to be the actual scene of the slaughter was discovered and the island became known as Massacre Island.) But the father and his two remaining sons carried on their great work.

La Vérendrye's course was clear. In order to have bases for further exploration and to pinch off the fur trade to the English (they were back on Hudson Bay), he had to build posts at just the right spots. He chose them with uncanny accuracy. By 1738 he had built Fort la Reine (near Poplar Point), on the Assiniboine, and Fort Rouge, in what is now Winnipeg.

The battle was joined and furs flowed to Montreal. But not in large enough quantities to satisfy his creditors. Between them and his jealous rivals he was always on the verge of losing his monopoly, and he had to make long, time-consuming trips back East to save it. Yet such obstacles could not stop him and his dedicated sons from probing for a route to the western Sea. They had heard glowing reports from the Crees of a tribe to the south called the Mandans, who cultivated corn and who told of a sea, far to the southwest, whose waters "are unfit to drink." La Vérendrye made the long journey, from Fort la Reine to the Mandan villages (near the present Bismark, North Dakota), but it proved to be a wild-goose chase.

Despite this discouraging first trip, the explorer's sons, Pierre and François, went back and probed deeper into the country. They were gone for a year. According to their journal, they got within sight of the "Shining Mountains"; but in 1913, a little girl living near Pierre, South Dakota, found a lead marker they had buried, so that it is fairly certain that they had reached only the Black Hills of South Dakota.

All through these years, obstructions from Montreal increased; and there were signs that the end was near. But La Vérendrye kept his mind focused on the great task, made plans far into the future; and he was still burning with zeal – at sixty-four – when the final blow fell. His enemies persuaded the French government to cancel his monopoly.

It was given to de Noyalles, a Court favourite, who soon showed that he couldn't manage the Indians. His successor, St. Pierre, couldn't either – and his sojourn in the West ended with a spectacular incident. One day when he was at Fort la Reine, two hundred Indians come through the gates and took possession of the fort. He used a novel way of getting rid of them: "I seized hold of a blazing brand, broke in the door of the powder magazine, knocked down a barrel of powder over which I passed the brand, telling the Indians . . . that in dying I would have the glory of subjecting them to the same fate . . . they fled."

The French threat to the English fur trade had little effect on the traders on the Bay; they hardly stirred in their sleep. And in 1759, on the Plains of Abraham, the British ended French rule in North America. The British fur trade had been saved by British arms.

CHAPTER 2

Battle for Beaver:
British vs. British (1763-1812)

Within a few years of the surrender of Canada by France, the HBC *faced a new threat. This time the Company couldn't be saved by British arms because the threat came from other British fur traders.*

Traders who had been working out of Albany, New York, saw the advantages of Montreal and many of them moved north. Canoe routes west from Montreal had been mapped out, and experienced French canoemen, the famous *voyageurs,* were willing to work for *les Anglais.* An efficient combination: British enterprise and capital coupled with French "know-how." Now the men of the Bay were going to have a fight on their hands.

It was an intriguing struggle, because most of the traders on both sides were British but not English – they were Scottish. It would be Scot against Scot. Moreover, most of the Scots were Highlanders, so the coming battle could be expected to have all the ferocity of a clan feud, but on an immensely larger stage.

The Nor'Westers. From the start, the Nor'Westers, as they came to be called (the HBC men called them "pedlars" till they were jolted into respect for them), were much more aggressive than were the Bay men. They had to be. The Bay men were salaried servants of the Company, so that they just had to *try* to get furs. The Nor'Westers had no company behind them; they had to raise money themselves, and raise enough to buy trade goods and equipment and to feed and pay their *voyageurs* for a whole year. So they *had* to get furs, or face ruin in one year.

But the Nor'Westers had one great advantage over the Bay men in dealing with the natives: they could leave much of the

24

actual trading to their *voyageurs*. These fellows seemed to understand and sympathize with the Indians, almost as if they were blood-brothers, as indeed many were. Their fathers had gone to the Northwest with La Vérendrye and his successors, and their mothers were Indian women whom their fathers had married there. They were the progenitors of the Métis. By contrast, the English company's employees, mostly Orkneymen, were dour and unimaginative and treated the "savages" with contempt. At most of the posts they even avoided contact with the Indians, dealing with them through windows.

For this and other reasons the Nor'Westers were so successful in intercepting the Indian fur brigades bound for the Bay that the HBC men finally awoke with a start. They sent Samuel Hearne into the up-country to establish their first inland post. Hearne was smart: he chose a spot at the very crossroads of the fur routes to the Bay – Cumberland Lake, west of The Pas – and there built Cumberland House. HBC posts followed at other strategic spots and the competitive placing of fur posts became a kind of giant chess game.

Samuel Hearne and His Nightmare Experiences. When the Governor of Fort Prince of Wales, Moses Norton – one of the few half-breeds to rise high in the HBC ranks – heard stories from the Indians of a northern river, which they said had copper mines on it, he sent Hearne to find them. Hearne set out twice, and had to turn back twice. On the second trip he and his guides were reduced to eating burnt bones, rotten deerskin, and old shoes. Then an ancient Indian chief, Matonabbee, told him why. He explained to Hearne patiently that no expedition could come to any good without *squaws*. "Squaws," he said, "are made for labour," and each of them could haul as much as two men; also, they required little food, because "as they always act as cooks, the very licking of their fingers . . . is sufficient for their subsistence."

Hearne tried again, with Matonabbee as chief guide, and with squaws. He found the river, but no mines. His reward after an arduous journey was not copper mines, but a horrifying experience. He had to stand helplessly by and watch his Indians massacre a party of Eskimos – men, women and children – they had caught sleeping.

A few years later, Hearne succeeded Norton as Governor of

25

Fort Prince of Wales, after watching another distressing spectacle: Norton, on his deathbed, raving wildly and accusing Hearne and other officers present of trying to steal the affections of some of his many, many Indian wives. But the new young Governor was to have an even more harrowing experience. The HBC had failed to keep the fort manned by its complement of four hundred men; and one day in 1782, three French warships appeared. Hearne found himself with only forty men, and he gave up without firing a shot. Should he have? One historian says that he "showed moral courage . . . when to prevent the needless slaughter of his garrison . . . he surrendered." Another says, "The Governor had a weak garrison and a weaker heart." Whatever the truth, he ordered his white tablecloth hoisted up the flagstaff and the "impregnable" fort was quickly impregnated by Frenchmen.

The Frenzy for Furs Brings Degradation to the Indians. It was the Indians who suffered most from the fur-trade competition. They would have suffered even more if it hadn't been for the missionaries. Since the days of Champlain these selfless men had followed the traders, often moving fearlessly ahead of them. A trader once reported that, in territory where the Indians were on the warpath, he was trying to sneak past a camp at night when suddenly he heard singing: the Indians were singing "Onward Christian Soldiers." A missionary was there or had been, and the trader knew he was safe.

The missionaries noted many admirable qualities in the Indian. One told of a squaw, whose husband had been killed, paddling the hundreds of miles to York Factory to pay his debts with furs. Another reported overhearing a chief say to a brave, who wanted to leave some furs with him: "They're safe – not a white man within a hundred miles!" Years later, in the 1820's, another wrote that the Indians were "always ready to alleviate misery"; that the Saulteaux "kept the Swiss settlers from starving – even though they knew that these new arrivals detested them."

The Indians had a strong liking for the white man's tobacco, but they loved his tea much more. The squaws, it seems, almost lived on tea. Some would drink it with salt; others would put fat in it, and then chew on the fat. One missionary wrote that the weight of tea consumed during the winter in one camp of Crees was twice that of the tobacco used.

But liquor was the great demoralizer. The traders on both sides seem to have regarded the Indian not as a human being but as a sort of mechanism whose sole function was to spring furs from beaver trap to trader's pile. And as the mechanism worked better when oiled with liquor, the traders in their frenzy for furs exploited the natives' frenzy for fire-water. An Indian chief is quoted as saying: "It is the prospect of a drink in the spring, enabling us to communicate freely with each other, that carries us through the winter and induces us to work so hard." The results of this exploitation – degradation, debauchery, even murder – didn't seem to bother the traders. Douglas MacKay in his history of the HBC says that most of them simply rationalized the situation: "The Indians don't have to trade for rum, so the debauchery is their fault. Our competitors use it, so we have to."

Not all the Nor'Westers were so obsessed by the fur mania that they regarded the Indian as merely a means to an end. David Harmon, though a New Englander of Puritan upbringing, took an Indian wife and had fourteen children. When eventually he decided to return home, he found that his love for his family would not permit his leaving them. And he took wife and children with him. John McDonnell took his woman too, and married her forty-six years after he began living with her.

Recent research, especially that of scientist Peter Farb, indicates that the most primitive Indian tribes had developed cultures far beyond what previously had been imagined; that through some twenty thousand years many tribes had evolved complex and most viable forms of social organization; that if in recent centuries they hadn't been exploited, demoralized, and almost destroyed by the white man, whom they had at first greeted as a god, they might have worked out in time a unique North American civilization.

Alexander MacKenzie and Alexander Henry. Alexander Mackenzie, like La Vérendrye, was fascinated by the dream of finding a route to the western Sea. And he found one – a North-West passage by land. On his way west from Montreal he made another discovery, one of special interest to Manitobans. At Lac du Bonnet on the Winnipeg River he reported boulder mosaics – rocks, some weighing several hundred pounds, laid out to form patterns or represent living creatures. Boulder mosaics can be seen in the Whiteshell today, some of them in the form of snakes three hundred feet long and others shaped like birds, fish, turtles and men up to ninety feet long. When or why or by whom they were made, no one knows; but one archaeologist suggests that it might have been as long as seven thousand years ago. The Indians through the centuries have no doubt looked on them as divine creations, and apparently some Indians today still remain somewhat in awe of them. A 95-year-old native, when queried, said, "They know if they go near them they die!"

Another Nor'Wester, Alexander Henry the younger, kept a journal which, except for two short periods, he wrote up every evening until midnight. It ends with an unfinished sentence – a day before he was drowned. In the journal he gives some examples of Indian first-aid practice. Once when a child fell in a fire, the father pounded and chewed a certain root and bark and spat the resulting medication on the burns. (Perhaps it healed them, but Henry couldn't wait to find out.) Another time, when a man bit off a fellow brave's nose in a drunken brawl, the victim's friends found the gory bit of flesh and bandaged it back on. (Henry was probably glad not to have been able to check on the success of this operation.) He was often impressed with Indian common sense and inventiveness. Once, when a horse got stuck up to its belly in mud, they cut quantities of long grass and pushed it under the horse until the horse was freed.

Henry himself was pretty inventive. Having bought two saddle horses from a roving band of Indians at "The Forks" for "a nine-gallon keg of mixed rum each," he found that these members of the Snakes tribe had gypped him: the horses turned out to have sore backs. He had to have his supplies and furs transported, so during ensuing seasons evolved that most typical of western symbols, the Red River cart. If it was not the first, it was certainly one of the earliest.

At Henry's Pembina post a few years later, another kind of history was made. One day a young Nor'Wester, Jean Baptiste Lagimodière, arrived with his wife. Anne-Marie Lagimodière had travelled all the way from Quebec, prepared to share her husband's hardships in the Wild West. She was not the first recorded white woman on the prairies, but she was the first to raise a family there. One of her grandchildren was Louis Riel. Anne-Marie started her family at Pembina, early in January, 1808, when she gave birth to a baby girl, the second white child born on the prairie.

Other Nor'Westers also kept journals, at least intermittently. There are various oddities found in their writings: *voyageurs* were fanatically proud of their prowess – they could paddle seventy miles in a day. Once, two canoes raced for two days without a *voyageur* leaving his canoe. . . . Canoemen were generally short of stature, but one was a giant Negro named Bonga. His Indian wife also gave birth to a child at Henry's fort. . . . Trader John McKinnon sneered when he heard that Henry had taken in a bear cub as a pet. But one day a motherless buffalo calf followed him into his fur post and he found he simply couldn't turn it away. . . .

The shortage of food was one of the hazards the traders had to contend with, and they often bought Indian dogs for meat. Sometimes flocks of passenger pigeons, "so numerous they blocked out the sun," would roost nearby, hundreds to a tree – "the very branches snapped under their weight." They could be knocked over with a stick. . . .

One of the Nor'Westers' mottoes was, "When among wolves, howl!" Some were so intoxicated with profit that they traded the buttons off their own coats. If a drunken Indian threatened to become violent, a trader might lace his next drink with laudanum to put him to sleep. Once during a brawl at Eagle Hills fort, a trader put in too much laudanum; the Indian died – and his friends stabbed ten traders to death. . . .

An Indian once trapped a most unusual kind of beaver – an albino. It had pink toenails and pink scales on its tail. . . . And a Nor'Wester, visiting an HBC factor – on June 5 – found him reading the morning *London Times* – dated June 5. The factor explained. Receiving mail only once a year, he always had the morning *London Times* for the whole previous year sent to him. And so each morning he could read the "news" – exactly one year late.

The Nor'Westers Unite. By 1780, life had become a nightmare for the Nor'Westers. Even though some of them had worked their way into distant, new fur fields, they were beginning to realize that they would kill the goose that laid the golden egg unless they worked together to keep it alive. So in 1783, the great majority of traders united to form the North West Company.

It took another twenty years to get the bugs out of the new organization, and to persuade all the traders to join. Once this

had been accomplished it became an efficient and extraordinarily successful company. The chief reason, no doubt, was that the men who spent the winter trading for furs were not just salaried employees, like the HBC men, but were "wintering partners" – sharing in their company's profits. Every summer they met the Montreal partners – the moneyed men – at their big fur and supply exchange depot on the western shore of Lake Superior. In 1803, the Pigeon River route location was abandoned in favour of the Kamonistiquia River in order to avoid paying U.S. taxes.

This combination of social gathering and shareholders' conference became the highlight of the year. First there was a "sound of revelry by night" – every night – in the huge banqueting hall: boisterous drinking and carousing, uproarious stories, amid raucous laughter, of outwitting the "ancient and mummified" HBC. (One of their jokes was, "HBC stood for 'Here Before Christ.'") But during the day, these men, whom someone has described as "hard-living and hard-drinking, hard as nails in business and cool as ice," spent long hours in mapping out plans and campaigns. Then, each man having received his share of the year's profits, they took off east and west.

By 1810, the North West Company was so successful that the HBC monopoly had become next to meaningless. One reason for its success was that its aggressive traders had gotten in behind the Bay men and beaten them into the fur-rich Athabasca country and on to the West Coast. Of course, the longer the NWC extended its transport lines, the more vital food became. But the Nor'Westers had taken this into account and had developed a magnificent system by which there would always be a dependable supply of food for all their posts and crewmen west of Lake Superior.

An important crossroads in this food-supply system was at the forks of the Red and Assiniboine, a bottleneck through which much east-west or north-south traffic passed. And near the forks could be found the outliers from the immense buffalo herds of the prairies. The Indians had long mastered the organized buffalo hunt, but the Métis, now numerous, had improved on it. The result was that pemmican – said to have been the most nourishing single item of diet even known – could be produced in quantity. Vast tonnages were prepared for both fur companies.

Today it is hard to realize how vital pemmican had become to the far-ranging fur brigades and wide-spread posts. There was

31

simply no other adequate food supply available. If the NWC's life line were ever cut it would mean disaster. No one thought that that could ever happen. Nevertheless the Nor'Westers were soon to receive a jolt more threatening than any they had delivered to the Hudson's Bay Company.

CHAPTER 3

Our First Farmers
and the Fur War (1812-1821)

The HBC *just wanted to enjoy its monopoly and pay bigger and bigger dividends. The* NWC *just wanted to get the bulk of the furs so that all the partners could retire early – and rich. Then along came Lord Selkirk in the early 1800's to spoil this good clean competition by planting a colony in the heart of the fur country! The result? A three-way conflict. The outcome? The best man, or men, did not win – at least not on merit. Geography decided the winner.*

Thomas Douglas was a seventh son; he became the Earl of Selkirk only after his father and six brothers had died. He had long pitied the Scottish and Irish crofters who were being driven off their little farms by their landlords, their former clan chieftains; raising sheep was more profitable to the owners than tenant farming. Believing he could relieve some of the suffering, the Earl tried to persuade the HBC directors to allow him to settle some of the homeless families on a wee corner of their vast Rupert's Land. Silly request! How would that increase dividends? Fortunately he had money and powerful relatives who sympathized with his concern for the crofters. Selkirk's group simply proceeded to buy up HBC shares until they owned a forty-per-cent interest in the Company. That was enough for the good lord's purpose and he persuaded the directors to make him a grant of land. It was quite a grant: the whole Red River Valley, an area five times as large as all Scotland and extending into the present Minnesota and North Dakota. (For this he paid the HBC a nominally legal ten shillings and undertook, among other conditions to provide it with "200 servants yearly.") The area was to be known as Assiniboia, and as its first local Governor, Selkirk appointed a military man, Miles Macdonnell.

Of course the Nor'Westers were outraged, and they used their considerable influence to try to stop the "eccentric Lord's mad scheme." They believed they were justified: this was nothing but a plot by the HBC to ruin them. It is true that the project was not purely philanthropic; the young, idealistic Selkirk was also a practical businessman. He and his supporters used their influence to secure the adoption of a policy of aggressive competition against the NWC and protection for the colonists.

"Un-British" Tactics Discourage Settlers. Selkirk's troubles really began with the securing of settlers. His enemies resorted to sheer skullduggery to dissuade people from going to "the Land of Cold," as some of their agents labelled it. With many of the prospects the propaganda worked. Some, even after going aboard ship, changed their minds, and a few leaped into the water and fled to the hills. Some HBC officials were as opposed to the scheme as were the Nor'Westers, and were covertly obstructive. For instance, for the first ship in the Company's history to carry human freight rather than trade goods, they provided the *Edward and Ann*, a sorry craft, and a badly manned one; three of the crew were small boys.

The voyage, in the summer of 1811, of this party (all workmen) was a harrowing experience. It took sixty-one days, the longest trip to York Factory on record, and the ship landed too late in the season for the men to start inland. They couldn't have anyway, because, unbelievable as it sounds, the petty officers had quarrelled over the landing of the river boats that had been sent along with the men to take them to Red River. Instead, the boats were actually returned to Scotland. After a heart-breaking winter, part of it encamped in log huts hurriedly erected, the workmen embarked on their hazardous journey: 728 miles of turbulent rivers and dangerous rapids, with forty or fifty portages. They succeeded by the most heroic effort in reaching Red River in fifty-five days, at the end of August, 1812.

Our "Pilgrim Fathers" Have a Mixed Reception. The arrival of the "Pilgrim Fathers" of Western Canada was an important event in Canadian history. Governor Macdonnell accordingly performed a fitting ceremony. The Nor'Westers' post, Fort Gibraltar, was on

34

the west bank of the Red and its strength and name were so obviously symbolic of the Montreal company's attitude that it might as well have carried the sign: "All settlers who enter our fur reserve, beware!" The Governor held the ceremony on the east bank (later St. Boniface), and he invited three NWC "gentlemen," several free Canadians (French-speaking) and a group of Indians. The historic moment came when he directed the patent of Lord Selkirk to his vast concession to be read, and "delivering and seizing" were "formally taken." Then, simply as a courtesy to the free Canadians, but also of some historical interest, he had some parts translated into French. There was also the appropriate pageantry: colourful uniforms, flags flying, and cannon (both Lord Selkirk's and the HBC's) discharging in a grand salute.

But the immigrants were probably not impressed, and for a good reason. They had already learned that although the HBC men in the area had had orders to make preparations for them, absolutely nothing had been done. Not even a bag of pemmican had been set aside for them. So they had to spend the winter at Pembina, seventy miles to the south; and so did the other men, women and children in the parties that came out during the next four years. Historian George Bryce tells of the ordeal of the families just in getting to Pembina.

The Indians, he says, seemed friendly (they were, and they remained so through the years), so Macdonnell persuaded a band of Saulteaux to guide the marchers. "The caravan was grotesquely comical . . . the Indians on their "shaganappi" ponies . . . men, women and children trudging wearily on foot." (This was comical? To whom?) "The Indians were kind . . . but the Redman loves a joke and often indulges in horse-play." The horse-play consisted of an "I-want-that" Indian game: a Highlander would have to hand over the gun his father had carried at Culloden, a women her wedding ring. And the braves, who "loved a joke," laughed at the women when they grew so tired they begged for a ride; the Manitou had decreed that squaws should walk.

The Famous "Long March." A nightmarish experience afflicted the 1814 party even before it arrived at Red River. Typhoid broke out on shipboard and even the ship's doctor came down with it. One of the passengers, Kate McPherson, became a veritable Florence Nightingale. The captain disembarked his passengers – men, women and children – at Churchill instead of **York** Factory where accommodation and inland boats awaited them. There they spent a terrible winter, some of them living in tents. The HBC officials are said to have been quite harsh with them, even confiscating their gun-locks so they wouldn't shoot "the Company's partridge!" Many died.

In the early spring, 1815, twenty-one men and twenty women – the others were too weak – set out to walk the 150 miles to York Factory on snowshoes; starting to the skirl of the bagpipes on a march that every descendent of the Selkirk settlers is rightly proud to relate.

In the group was a pregnant woman, Mrs. Jean McKay. One day she and her husband Angus, with a brother, a sister-in-law, an Indian guide, plus three or four others, dropped out of the line long enough for baby Selkirk McKay to be born on the trail. He survived the rigours of the weather and the trip, living for over "three-score" years. When the reunited marchers finally reached Red River, the ordeal for two of them ended in romance: Kate McPherson and Alexander Sutherland were married. A hundred years later, one of her descendants in Winnipeg, Mrs W.R. Black, still owned Kate's New Testament. Stitched into its faded brown silk ribbon are the words: "Lord Teach Me to Pray."

The Settlers' Governor Riles the Nor'Westers. For a year and a half after the first settlers arrived, neither the Nor'Westers nor the Métis showed much hostility; in fact, the Nor'Westers sold the settlers food on occasion, charging it to Selkirk. What set the heather afire was a drastic move, not by the fur traders, but by Governor Macdonnell. Selkirk had warned him not to do anything that might arouse the hostility of the Nor'Westers. But Macdonnell did just that, in 1814, by posting a proclamation which stated that, because of the necessity of conserving food in the area for the many people in his care, no provisions were to be taken out of Assiniboia for a year. (The 1812-1814 war had seriously affected incoming supplies from the east for the Nor'-Westers, who consequently would need extra local food farther west.)

The Métis were aghast, puzzled, furious. It meant that they would not be allowed to "run" the usual number of buffalo in the territory. They could sell supplies only to Macdonnell or his

36

agents. The proclamation naturally made the Nor'Westers see red too. To them this was clearly a deliberate attempt to starve out their Western posts. Shortly afterwards, the Governor added fuel to the fire. Declaring that the Nor'Westers at Fort la Souris had disobeyed his proclamation, he had his men go to the post and seize several hundred bags of pemmican. Such high-handed action bore the inevitable result: plans were laid by the Nor'Westers to break up the new settlement.

Two-thirds of the Colonists Are "Persuaded" to Settle in Canada. One of the Montreal partners, Duncan Cameron, was sent out to soften up the settlers. Cameron was an expert at it. A Scot, he had been a captain in the War of 1812, and he appeared at Red River dressed in his scarlet military tunic. Fluent in Gaelic, he posed as a friend, ingratiated himself with the colonists, and stirred them up against the Selkirk "tyranny"; so successfully that some of the settlers even broke open Macdonnell's storehouse and removed the colony's nine small cannons.

Then the loyal colonists were subjected to a war of nerves: they were fired on by unseen marksmen and their houses were attacked. When Cameron decided that they had been sufficiently softened up he made them a tempting offer: free transportation to new homes in Upper Canada. Two-thirds of the families accepted, and a party of some 140 men, women and children underwent the harrowing journey. Although they left the Red River peril far behind them, they still had to start life all over again. And some of the promises made to them were never fulfilled.

The Colony "Knocked on the Head." Cameron had accompanied these disgruntled settlers, but the thirteen families that refused his offer were to suffer even more at the hands of Nor'Wester Alexander Macdonnell, who was a cousin of Governor Macdonnell. The Nor'Westers had long been working on the Métis, chiefly by appealing to their pride. They were "different," the traders told them. Being partly Indian, they had a stake in the land; and being partly white, with the qualities of the whites, they were a "new nation." And they couldn't trust the HBC men, who were not only English but Protestant to boot. (Ironically, most of the Nor'Westers were Protestants, too.) As for these settlers, wouldn't they drive away the buffalo if they were allowed to

38

stay? And hadn't their Governor already tried to stop buffalo hunting? So the Nor'Wester Macdonnell had no trouble turning a band of the wilder spirits loose on the settlement. Led by young Cuthbert Grant, "Captain" of the Métis, they burned down cabins and terrorized the remaining settlers until they too left, all except for the HBC fishing post, Jack River, on Lake Winnipeg. The Red River colony, on which so much hope had been expended, had now been, as one Nor'Wester wrote gloatingly, "knocked on the head."

But, as the saying goes, it takes more than that to kill a Scot. John McLeod, the HBC trader at the Forks, and two Company servants, refused to leave. They turned the little blacksmith shop into a fort and (according to one report) cut up logging chain into shrapnel splinters, rammed them into the one small cannon they had and, all their Highland blood aflame, prepared for battle. All we know is that the blacksmith shop wasn't burned down, that its defenders didn't leave, and that the Métis did.

Before the summer was over, Colin Robertson, a former Nor'Wester now in Selkirk's service, arrived at Jack River from Montreal. He brought the banished colonists back to the ruined settlement. They found McLeod and his men tending an abundant and ripening harvest. But the canny Robertson knew that if the colony was going to survive it would have to have a military force to protect it. And having been informed in the East that Selkirk himself was coming to Montreal from England that fall, he persuaded Jean Baptiste Lagimodière to undertake a journey east with the story of the colony's plight.

Lagimodière's Epic Journey to Montreal. According to a record of the time, the Lagimodière family lived in a loop of the Assiniboine, today occupied by the St. Charles Country Club. Moving his wife Anne-Marie and the children into Fort Douglas, on October 15, 1815, Jean Baptiste set out with an HBC man and an Indian guide. They accompanied him only as far as Sault Ste. Marie. But he made it east from there travelling alone over unknown trails. His journey had been regarded quite rightly as an example of the triumph of courage over adversity. A famous painting shows Lagimodière, dressed in his leather woodsman's clothes, walking up to Selkirk at a Montreal ball, carrying in his hand the dispatches containing the disturbing news.

The delayed return journey was a nightmare. Apparently the

Nor'Weste.. at Fort William had found out he was on the way back because east of the fort Lagimodière and his men were attacked, beaten, and robbed by a Negro interpreter and ten Indians. Their assailants got what they were apparently sent to get: papers entrusted to Jean Baptiste by Selkirk. And they robbed them of everything else they had, even the dainty gifts Jean Baptiste had bought for Anne-Marie, among them a silk handkerchief, a necklace, and a little mirror. The four captured men were taken to Fort William, where Lagimodière was put into solitary confinement. The three companions were cast adrift on the lake without musket or ammunition, and were found two weeks later, half starved.

Seven Oaks: A Needless Massacre. Shortly after Robertson brought the settlers back from Lake Winnipeg, a fifth party from the British Isles arrived with a new Governor, another military man, Robert Semple. They found the restored "old" settlers, despite the fact their homes were in ashes, rejoicing in a glorious harvest. But that winter there were rumours that the Nor'Westers and their henchmen, the Métis, were planning "the most diabolical scheme for the utter extermination of the colony." By March, evidence mounted; on June 17, two Saulteaux from the west warned Semple that a war party of Métis was advancing to attack the colony. Yet when their Chief, Peguis, offered help, the inexperienced Governor declined it. He continued encouraging the settlers to go out and work on their farms, some of which were two miles from the fort.

He clearly failed to understand the situation, acting as if he were the Governor of an African colony. In Africa, if the "natives" revolted, one would simply "show the flag," the symbol of authority, and they would prostrate themselves in awe. Semple actually stated that he "had a paper" which he would show any attackers. That would jolly well put them in their place! Not all agree with the historian who declared that Semple was a "pompous ass." But most people would agree with Bryce that he "had eyes but saw not."

On June 19, 1816 – two days after the Saulteaux warning – the blow fell. A band of sixty or seventy mounted and armed Métis, organized at Qu'Appelle under Cuthbert Grant – only twenty-three, but already an unquestioned leader – swept down the Assiniboine to where St. James-Assiniboia is now. At

Omand's Creek, Grant struck across the prairie north-eastward to meet (so it was claimed later) a party of eastern Nor'Westers on the Red some miles north of Fort Douglas. It is thought that swampy ground made them swerve closer to the fort than they had originally intended. When about a mile and a half from the fort they saw a group of men leave it and walk towards them. It was Semple with his five officers and about twenty men (all but one, John McLean, servants of the HBC). It has been described as a group too large for a parley, but too weak and poorly equipped for a fight.

They met at Seven Oaks, about three-quarters of a mile from the fort, and Semple called out, "What do you want?" At this, one of the Métis, Boucher, rode towards the Governor. There were hot words. Semple tried to seize Boucher's bridle, and a shot rang out. (The Coltman investigating commission would later decide that "next to a certainty" it came from one of Semple's party. This is disputed by witnesses at the time.) Another shot was fired and another, and in far less time than it took them to come from the fort, Semple and nineteen of his party were dead.

This was the so-called "Battle" of Seven Oaks. The mental state of the settlers at the fort after the slaughter can be imagined. And as if the shock were not already almost unbearable, the bodies of the dead were left on the fields to be torn to pieces by birds and animals. (One of the wounded, John Bourke, was brought in – undoubtably saved from death – by Chief Peguis's Saulteaux.) The Métis took over Fort Douglas, and at the order of Cuthbert Grant the settlers were packed into boats, and once more banished to Jack River. Among the victors there was rejoicing and hilarity; now the "new nation" had proved itself! And the Métis bard, Pierre Falcon, celebrated the "triumph" of the *Bois Brûlés* in victory verse.

Many of those with Grant were later brought to trial but none was ever punished. Commissioner Coltman decided that it had been an "accidental battle" in a "private war," and that therefore individuals should not be charged with homicide. According to historian Alexander Ross, retribution caught up with no less than twenty-six of the sixty-two in the party. Within a few years, he says, they all suffered "sudden or violent deaths." And he tells when and where and how, in each case, in what he calls his "melancholy catalogue."

The Colony Is Restored by Selkirk. At Fort William the partners were still celebrating the "good" news about Seven Oaks when bad news arrived: Lord Selkirk himself was on the way from Montreal with some one hundred Swiss mercenaries, men of the de Meuron regiment, who had been brought to Canada for possible use in the War of 1812.

When Selkirk heard about the massacre he changed his course, descended on Fort William, and seized it. In his authorized capacity as a Canadian magistrate, he arrested seven of the chief traders. He billeted his own men there for the winter, but in December he sent a small force to recapture Fort Douglas. (The men were led, incidentally, by John Tanner, a "white Indian," who had been kidnapped by the Indians as a child.) It took seven weeks of walking in bitterly cold weather, but at last they reached the fort – in the middle of the night. There were no sentries posted, and as Tanner reported later: "We made a ladder in the way the Indians make them, by cutting the trunk of a tree, with the limbs trimmed long enough to serve to step on; and placing it against the wall, we went over." The rest was easy. So now the Nor'Westers at both Fort William and Fort Douglas were prisoners. Their celebrating had been premature.

In the late spring of 1817, Selkirk went to his Red River colony. This was the first and only time he ever saw it, and he devoted the summer to putting the colonists back on their feet. He also persuaded the Indians to sign a treaty by which, in return for an annual gift of "good marketable tobacco," they would turn over to "The Silver Chief," as they called him, their claim to the land along the Red and Assiniboine. This was probably the happiest time Lord Selkirk had experienced since the founding of his colony; certainly that was true of his sorely tried people.

But the happiness didn't last. A curse seemed to rest on the land. In the fall, a heavy frost and a violent storm destroyed the crop they had sown with axe and hoe. They were thankful to have buffalo meat, supplied chiefly by the Métis, supplemented by wild "vegetables," such as the prairie turnip and a weed called "fat hen." The following year much of the crop was devoured by grasshoppers, which settled on the fields several inches deep. The following spring the larvae the insects had deposited in the ground turned into grasshoppers in such vast numbers that they smothered fires, poisoned the water, and left not even a

42

blade of grass for hay. And what was worse, the settlers, searching desperately on hands and knees, couldn't even find enough grains of wheat for seeding the next spring.

They had to have seed, so in January a party of volunteers set off southward along the river on snowshoes, with dog-teams and toboggans. For three months they plodded on wearily, and after 750 miles of blizzards, slush, and floods they reached their objective, Prairie du Chien on the Mississippi. There they bought seven and a half tons of seed wheat. They bought lumber, too, and built flatboats in which to carry their precious cargo. They fought their way back against swollen currents till they reached the short portage into the Red, and then rode home on its brimming current. The wheat, though planted late, grew to harvest without disaster; as well it might – by the time it reached the settlement it had cost Lord Selkirk twenty dollars a bushel. Oddly enough, Prairie du Chien was to be paid back some seed wheat – forty years later. The first known record of grain exported from Red River is of four sacks of seed wheat shipped in 1860 – to Prairie du Chien.

Lack of Spiritual Guidance. The Selkirk settlers never complained when they were without food; but the Presbyterians, which meant most of the people, remonstrated, and with justice, that they were being deprived of spiritual food. That is, they had no minister. They pleaded and petitioned, year after year, for one to be sent out. A minister of their faith finally did arrive – *in 1851!*

If a handful of Presbyterians in the wilds of America were not considered very important, even fewer Anglicans were more fortunate. In 1820, the Rev. John West was sent out to them. As for the Catholics, Lord Selkirk, who was a Protestant, completed arrangements with the Quebec hierarchy, and in 1818, Father Provencher and Father Dumoulin arrived – in style. They were honoured guests among the *voyageurs* in a flotilla of canoes.

The Fathers' first little church and school was built on the east bank to serve the Métis and the de Meurons. With a few immigrant families from Quebec arriving that same year, it marked the beginning of the city of St. Boniface, on land donated by the Scottish lord.

Incidentally, the name St. Boniface is not French. The de Meurons had a French name and they were mostly Swiss; but they spoke German and were the largest group on the east bank. So, in an admirable gesture, the Fathers called the church after the English missionary, Boniface, who many years before had become the "Apostle of Germany."

The de Meurons didn't deserve the honour. Being mercenaries, they apparently lacked the simple virtues valued in all countries. They were all bachelors, and although there were fewer than seventy of them they made up for lack of numbers by their rapacity. Almost to a man they were, according to a writer of the time, "quarrelsome, slothful, famous bottle companions, and ready for any enterprise however lawless."

A few years after the arrival of the professional soldiers a "sunburst," as Bryce puts it, appeared on their horizon: a considerable number of Swiss families landed at Red River – with "a plenty of handsome daughters." When the new families were placed in tents alongside them, the bachelors were ecstatic. Bryce says that "the description of the way in which the de Meurons invited families having young women in them to their wifeless cabins was ludicrous," and that "the families which had no daughters were left to languish in their comfortless tents." Comment seems superfluous, except to say that the families that "languished" probably decided before long that they were the lucky ones.

Geography Decides the Winner. The Battle of Seven Oaks was followed by three other "battles," all of them lasting about five years. First there was the colonists vs. a new and unbelievably irresponsible Governor, another Alexander Macdonnell. This man was nicknamed the "Grasshopper Governor" for he was "as great a destroyer within doors as the grasshoppers in the field." The second battle was Lord Selkirk vs. the NWC in the courts. Selkirk found that in both Canada and England the Nor'Westers' influence was such that he could never hope to obtain juctice. Broken in health and purse, he retired from the struggle and died in 1820 at the age of forty-nine.

The third battle was the HBC vs. the NWC in the fur fields, where ruthless competition had erupted into open war. Traders ambushed those of the other company, took each other prisoner, and regarded captured furs as spoils of war. The HBC's Orkneymen had learned the tricks of the trade used by their rivals and had adopted their aggressive spirit. In 1819, they delivered their enemies a body blow. With an armed schooner and a company of de Meurons (they had to be good for something) a party of HBC men waylaid the NWC's brigades at the portage of the Grand Rapids near the mouth of the Saskatchewan and seized a fortune in furs. This was perhaps the straw that broke the camel's back: at the very least, the merchant princes of Montreal now knew that their organization, which had flashed across the sky like a brilliant meteor, was now going to crash.

The end came in 1821. One day, out of the blue, it was announced that the two companies had "amalgamated." Every effort was made to dress up the transaction as a reasonable compromise, but the bitter truth the Nor'Westers had to swallow was that the old company had triumphed; or rather, geography had triumphed, for not even the skill and drive of one of the most efficient trading organizations ever devised could overcome the elemental fact of distance: the Nor'Westers' line of communication was too long. They could have prolonged the life of their company simply by encouraging the settlers, since the colony would shortly have provided food for all, and other food besides pemmican. But unable to take the long view, and angered by settlers "invading" their fur preserve, they had gone stubbornly ahead to their own destruction.

CHAPTER 4

Profits vs. People (1821-1849)

For the people of Red River – an island in a fur-trading ocean – the union of the battling companies promised the end of violence and a new era. A period of peace and relative prosperity did begin, but living under the HBC monopoly the settlers lacked those fundamental freedoms which they had to come to find, like the millions of other immigrants to the New World: the freedom to grow, make, buy, and sell in a free market; and to share in making the laws they were expected to obey.

The Company's empire, stretching from Labrador to Vancouver Island, was ruled by the "Little Emperor," George Simpson. He ruled his half-continent efficiently – never were dividends higher! And since that was his job – to produce peak profits – his rule of the people was conditioned by it. His attitude was autocratically paternal: "Father knows best." Which really meant – "what's best for the HBC."

And so, although the violence of the fur war had ended, a new conflict had begun. Red River was living, as historian W.L. Morton says, "in uneasy balance between civilization and barbarism, the river lot and the buffalo hunt." Would it win the right to work out its own destiny? Who would win the war – profits or people? Only time would tell.

If the members of the HBC's London Committee had had any sense of history they would have seen to it that their fur post at Red River was named Fort Selkirk. But they didn't. In 1821, Nicholas Garry, one of the committeemen, came out from England to make the transition from competition to monopoly as smooth as possible. He had Fort Gibraltar rebuilt; and the new Governor, George Simpson, named it – naturally – Fort Garry. Lower Fort Garry would follow in the 1830's.

The great task before Garry and Simpson was deciding which of the nearly two hundred HBC and NWC posts should be closed and what personnel should be dispensed with. There was quite a house-cleaning: two-thirds of the men in the two companies were dismissed. More former NWC men were kept on than HBC men. And they were to prove as loyal as if they had always been Bay men. No doubt one chief reason was that the NWC co-operative principle had been adopted by the Bay: "servants" had become "partners."

Large numbers of former fur traders, especially Bay men, settled in Assiniboia. In fact, retired fur traders soon outnumbered settlers. They built homes, some of them most beautiful, at St. Andrew's and St. John's; so many of the Orkneymen among them took up land in St. James that it became known as "Orkneytown." These men brought their Indian wives and half-breed children with them; they had no more reason to be embarrassed by them there than they had had at their fur posts. An Indian wife might wear moccasins and smoke a pipe, but having practically run a fur post, she was capable of conducting her domestic affairs with competence and dignity. She proudly added her children to the mixed-blood majority in a community where only a small minority were "pure" white. And so she would have justifiably regarded hers as one of the "first families" of the Red River settlements. Indeed, such families became a unique aristocracy.

The "Little Emperor": Administrator and Showman. George Simpson was a red-headed Scot, short and stocky like a Napoleon, in his thirties, and with only one year's experience in the fur trade. He was bursting with energy, impatient of time and space, shrewd, keen, and observant. If he was sometimes a tyrant (an employee said he demanded "deference to the point of humility") he could also be most genial – he was often called the "Jolly Governor." Certainly a magnetic personality. Altogether, it is not surprising that he was able to persuade the London Committee that he was the strong man needed to weld the two factions into a smooth-running machine, and they gave him unprecedented power.

As for the Red River colony, he didn't bother consulting its people – he didn't believe in that wishy-washy "American thing," democracy. He reorganized the existing "Council of Assiniboia,"

47

and saw to it that its members were Company men, more interested in profits, than in people. In fact, Simpson once stated in a letter that "nearly every member is hostile to settlement."

One chief reason for his business effectiveness was that, like any live business manager, he visited his "branch offices" frequently. He practically lived in his canoe or on horseback, often turning up at a post a day before he was expected. Now at Moose Factory, then at York Factory – and often at Red River – he found out for himself how to advance the interests of the Company. In his very first year he travelled "by paddle and saddle" from Hudson Bay to the Pacific coast in eighty-four days.

His paddlers were hand-picked *voyageurs* and Iroquois, proud of their skill and their role. Sometimes, though, they became exasperated with Simpson's impatience for more speed. In fact, a much-told story of the Selkirk settlers has it that a stalwart *voyageur*, a favourite of the Governor's, once became so infuriated that "he seized the tormentor, who was small of stature, and with a plentiful supply of *Sacrés,* dipped him in the lake!" Apparently Simpson was "big" enough to "take it"; and he went on, year after year, covering astonishing stretches of water. He is said to have travelled between Montreal (now an HBC town) and Fort Garry forty times in his thirty-eight years' "reign." Later in his career, but still before the days of steamships and railways, he travelled around the world.

The arrival of Simpson's "flying-express" canoe brigade at a post was always a stage-managed "spectacular." His arrival at Norway House on one occasion is described by Bryce. That morning, as every morning, Simpson had had his men up at one, and "on the road" by two. They paddled until eight or nine, and then stopped for breakfast. And now, late in the day, the garishly painted and decorated canoes approached Norway House. But, while still a few miles off, the impresario gave a signal and the crew immediately pulled into shore. And the spot where they landed became an actor's dressing-room. The Governor, already elaborately dressed, prepared for his "entrance"; and his crewmen donned bright, feathered head-dress. When "curtain time" approached, the canoes, now aflutter with little flags, shot into the stream again; and in full career dashed through the deep gorge leading to the fort. Just within earshot of the audience, the piper in the first canoe delivered his strident strains. Then from

48

the second canoe came a staccato tattoo from the buglar; this was followed instantly by a rollicking boat-song from the *voyageur* paddlers. The post men knew their cues too; and in response to this fanfare, there was a roaring salute from the fort's cannon. When the first canoe touched land, out leaped two *voyageurs* selected for the privilege, and "His Excellency" was carried bodily to shore. All this, like the homecoming of a conquering hero, the audience loved – especially the "children" (the Indians). And it served the maestro's purposes: as an integral part of his imaginative way of keeping everybody happy, and thereby boosting the fur business.

Simpson's visits to Red River were indeed bright spots in the life of the colony. Says Bryce: "Old settlers tell how, when Sir George arrived, every grievance, disaster, suspicion, or bit of gossip was carried to him," and that "his patience and ingenuity were freely exercised in 'jollying' the people and giving them condescending attention." Perhaps it is to his credit that he took time for all this, although his mind probably never wandered far from business.

Like so many great men he sometimes let his mind wander – in the direction of a pretty face. Says Douglas MacKay in this regard: "Children born of swarthy mothers . . . gave rise to legendary tales of extramarital relations on the heroic scale." Of course, the mothers of these "bits of brown," as he called all children of mixed blood, would be proud to have them bear the Simpson name; and the Governor paid for the upbringing of all of them. In fact, he insisted that his officers follow the same "gentlemanly" course.

Cuthbert Grant: Leader of the Métis. Until recently, most history books have given a one-sided picture of Grant. They describe his leading the Métis at the Battle of Seven Oaks, but give little of his subsequent activities. Researchers, especially MacLeod and Morton, in their *Cuthbert Grant of Grantown,* have shown that he made a great contribution to Manitoba history.

Grant can hardly be considered a Métis in a genetic sense. His father was a Scot and a prominent Nor'Wester, stationed at Qu'Appelle. His mother was only partly Cree and apparently had little French blood. His father died when he was six and Cuthbert was taken to Montreal, baptized in the Presbyterian church, and given a good education. He returned to Qu'Appelle a "young gentleman," but he clearly favoured the NWC cause. He soon became the leader of the wildest of the younger Métis. Year by year their cause became more and more of an obsession with him. As MacLeod and Morton put it: "A youthful and impetuous loyalty to the Company and the Métis is the key to the part he played against the settlers." And the Nor'Westers let him do their dirty work.

After the 1821 union of the two companies, the Young Fellows, as the Nor'Westers had called "Grant's gang," begged him to lead them against the settlement again. He refused and vowed never again to lead them in lawless violence. At this point Simpson entered the scene. Apparently he made a point of seeing much of the "new" Grant, even taking him in his own canoe on a trip to Montreal. The Governor was impressed with him.

But then Simpson blundered; he had Grant appointed as a clerk – at Red River! In the heart of the colony he had twice harried out of existence! How could the settlers be expected to forgive so soon? Some of them didn't. Changed man or not, Grant was attacked, physically, and he had to leave. Then the Governor made a wiser move: he arranged that his protégé be granted land on the White Horse Plain, some fifteen miles west of the Forks on the north bank of the Assiniboine. Grant had become a settler himself!

Such was his influence (added to that of Provencher) on "his people" that within a few years nearly all the Métis from all over the prairies came to Red River and took up little patches of land on the White Horse Plain, which soon became known as Grantown, or on the southern fringe of St. Boniface (later St. Vital). Even the five hundred or more at Pembina moved north – which, for Simpson, did much to correct a potentially dangerous international situation. In 1817, the forty-ninth parallel boundary line had been agreed upon, which meant that not only Pembina, but fully half of Selkirk's original grant was now in the United States. This meant, in turn, that the HBC had no authority there. In fact, United States cavalry had turned back buffalo hunters from the north, and the Métis at Pembina had been attacked by the Sioux. Most of the Métis were forced north of the line. It was thus possible that Grant's increasing influence might result in the Métis actually becoming the defenders of the colony against the Sioux.

The Governor's hopes were realized. Not only had Grant established the first farming community of any size between the present Winnipeg and the Rockies – as MacLeod and Morton put it, "the Little Scotland of Kildonan was matched by the Little Canada of Grantown" – but the Métis, already the colony's indispensable suppliers of buffalo meat, had become its protectors! And for almost fifty years its people looked on Grantown, the Métis "captial," as a bulwark against the Sioux menace.

For thirty years after the union, Cuthbert Grant played a striking role, not only as the father of his people and the protector of the colony, but also as the benefactor of individuals and families. His "in" with the Governor made it possible for him to be a "trouble-shooter," a kind of ombudsman. One of his great interests was medicine, and he performed the role of doctor so effectively that some writers think that at some point he must have taken a year off to study medicine. Whenever people were stranded by a blizzard, he would travel any distance, with his medicine chest and food on a toboggan, to save them. And while this original Assiniboia country doctor was spending most of his waking hours helping people, he was also – with his left hand, so to speak –keeping peace between the Crees and the Assiniboines.

The settlers were grateful: one day in the 1880's a grandmother was introduced to a young man by the name of Cuthbert Grant, and on being told that he was the grandson of the Cuthbert Grant of the early days she said: "We never slept quiet in our beds until your grandfather and his brave Métis came to settle among us." No wonder that MacLeod and Morton suggest that our history "has always been distorted by a natural but unhistorical emphasis on Selkirk and his colonists," and that the role of the Métis "must be given its proper place."

Through the years, Grant filled a succession of offices. From 1828 on he was Warden of the Plains, his job being to prevent "illicit trade in furs." (This was the only one of his many roles of which the Métis did not approve.) Yet it seems that his absorbing interest – somewhat like the fanatical love of golf that a businessman today might have – was the buffalo hunt. He could be called the "scientific" hunter; he developed it to a degree of organized efficiency that amazed outsiders. A visiting army officer is quoted as having said that he was "sad" when he found he couldn't persuade the Métis to form a cavalry unit for his forces.

(He would have been sadder had he seen them lick the tar out of a superior force of Sioux in 1851.)

Grant had become a devout Roman Catholic, and it was chiefly through his aid to Bishop Provencher that Grantown became established as the parish of St. Francis Xavier. (The original church, built in 1833, is still there, as are some of the original hand-made chairs.) The settlement's founding father wasn't "religious" at all times, though. In fact, in his later years he fell a little from grace – was known to have killed a bottle of rum at a sitting, which was ironic because he had saved many a man from drunkenness. Ironic too was the fall from his horse in 1854 which killed him: he was a superb horseman.

Buffalo Hunting: An Art. The buffalo hunt attracted big-game hunters from all over the world. The hunt was organized on strict military lines with definite rules and heavy penalties. Perhaps the strictest rule was that no hunter could start towards a herd till the command was given. Ross says he watched four hundred hunters start at the word of command, and return to camp with the tongues of 1,475 buffalo. Something like a million pounds of meat were brought in from the 1840 hunt – from two to four million pounds were left on the field.

Father Belcourt, who accompanied many hunts in his spiritual capacity, wrote that he never ceased to wonder at the hunters' skill, especially the rapidity with which they could fire their guns: "It is not rare to see three buffalo brought down by the same hunter within four hundred yards. . . . In loading their guns, only the first bullet is rammed home; for the others, they cap, pour in powder, then, having the mouth full of balls, they let one of them fall into the gun; the saliva makes it stick to the powder in the bottom of the barrel. The horse is so well trained that when his master leans from one side to the other, he obeys instantly." Belcourt also tells of a band of hunters who drove a herd to the edge of a rock-strewn embankment – and went over with them. "Buffalo, horses, and horsemen were overturned and rolled about in confusion. . . . One can hardly see how any of them escaped being killed . . . one man, only, lost consciousness, but soon regained it." And the "game" went on. The excitement was still so great, says the priest, that he couldn't resist joining in: "I dashed into the midst of the hunters and brought down a cow."

Sometimes you couldn't bring down a cow because the herd

was made up of bulls only. Paul Kane, the Canadian artist, risked his life by taking part in such a battle; no wonder the buffalo in his paintings look so alive. Of course, the herds were usually mixed, in which case the bulls would gallantly try to form a guard around the cows. So, to get at the cows – the meat was less likely to have "the consistency of leather," as Belcourt put it – the hunters had to break through the guard, thereby turning a buffalo hunt unto a bull fight. And things sometimes happened that a bull-fight audience would have enjoyed. Once a hunter, tossed high in the air by a bull, landed – in trick cowboy style – on the back of another bull. And John McDougall, the Methodist missionary, reported this incident: two bulls, one on either side of him, charged at the same instant; his horse leaped forward and the bulls met head-on. This turned their anger from the horse and rider unto each other, and with the missionary as an audience, they backed up and gave a repeat performance. Then he shot both of them.

The buffalo herds were sometimes aided by nature in their battle with their human enemies. Once, lightning struck the barrel of McDougall's gun and his hair caught fire. He recovered quickly from the shock, he says, but his horse was "stupefied for days." Prairie fires were always a hazard to both hunter and hunted. One day a band of Indians set the prairie afire to drive a herd of buffalo into a pound they had prepared. But the wind changed, the Indians leaped on their horses to flee – and were incinerated to a man.

The Missionaries: Selfless Men. The only institution in Assiniboia that played a greater part in people's lives than the Buffalo hunt was the church. And whether or not you liked church services you went or became on outcast. The Roman Catholics were the most numerous group because the Métis were the most numerous, and Bishop Provencher's great work was made even more effective when the Grey Nuns began arriving from Quebec in the 1840's. (Their long white house, now St. Boniface Museum, is the longest-occupied house in Greater Winnipeg.)

The Protestant church was essentially the "Established" church, the Church of England. The first Anglican clergyman, Rev. John West, had refused to modify its ritual to accommodate the Presbyterians. So they attended his services, but adhered to their own practice of standing up to pray and sitting down to sing. West's successor, Rev. David Jones, did modify it, "at the hazard," wrote Ross, "of forfeiting his gown." The Presbyterians were still without a minister, and still bitter; perhaps this partly explains why 114 of the settlers emigrated to the States in 1835.

Ross was critical of all three Protestant denominations – Anglicans, Presbyterians, Methodists – especially concerning their work among the Indians. Instead of first trying to save their souls, the missionaries should have been working patiently at civilizing them and getting them established on their own little farms. As it was, Ross declared, the natives were just mumbling rituals that were meaningless to them; and even while they were accepting handouts they were snickering at the white man and his forms of worship.

There doesn't seem to be much evidence to support such strong views. Certainly the missionaries influenced Simpson (who at first resented their taking up space in his fur canoes) in moving towards the abolition of the sale of liquor to Indians (he drastically reduced the use of it). And few people, then or now, would be critical of the work of the missionary at Norway House, James Evans, who slaved for years with lead type – made from the lead found in tea chests – so that he could "make birch bark talk," in the Cree language. He also substituted tin for birch bark in the building of his canoe; for some time he travelled in his own tin canoe. Thirty years later, Lord Dufferin, the Governor General, said that Evans deserved a title and a monument in Westminster Abbey.

Evans's printing invention was a godsend to missionaries (you can still buy a Cree dictionary), but there were bound to be language difficulties; for one thing, the Crees had no word for things they had never seen. One missionary, planning to paint scriptural passages on his church windows, asked them for the word for "sea." They said "Winnipeg" – meaning the lake of that name. So today the windows declare that God made "heaven and earth, Winnipeg, and all that in them is."

The 1826 Flood. The Red River settlement was a far more pleasant place to live in after 1821 than it had been before the union. The settlers had had to wait until 1822, ten years after the first little band arrived, before their crops were good enough to provide food for all. It was the first year they didn't have to go to Pembina just to keep eating. Then, for three years, things got better and better. In 1825, John Pritchard (one of the five or six of Semple's men who survived Seven Oaks) wrote: "The settlement now extends from White Horse Plain to Netley Creek. . . . We have an abundance of cattle . . . and the prospect of wheat exceeding anything heretofore produced." They did get a bumper crop and the settlers began to dare to think that maybe the land wasn't cursed after all.

But the next year another disaster struck the settlement. On May 2, the river rose nine feet – which brought a shocked "Yea Ho!" from the Indians. By May 5, the settlement was a lake. Several days later the lake was "seventeen miles wide and thirty-five feet above common river level." People fled to higher ground – Sturgeon Creek, Bird's Hill, Stony Mountain – and almost every house was swept into Lake Winnipeg. One house caught fire and it drifted along, half of it burning furiously, the other half submerged. Ross says that he and some others saw a man "who had two oxen tied together, with his wife and four children fixed on their backs. The terrified animals waded or floated as best they could . . . while the poor man, with a long line in his hands, kept before them. We got them to a place of safety." There were many such narrow escapes; fortunately there was only one death from drowning.

The vital problem was food; and the conniving de Meurons took advantage of the situation. The settlers had immediately driven their cattle to distant higher ground, and now, because of the water, they couldn't get back to them. But the de Meurons – who hardly possessed an animal of their own – could, and did. Says Ross: "They fed us with our own beef at 3d a pound . . . and these were the boys who had been brought to the country to restore the settlement to order and to keep the peace." When the waters went down – as fast as they had risen – the de Meurons remained in character; all but two left for the States. Many of the Swiss settlers left too, among them a young artist, Peter Rindisbacher, whose paintings are still highly prized.

A Peaceful, Pastoral Life. Before the flood, the people settled around the Forks had begun to work out a unique way of life, cut off as they were from the nearest civilized community (which at that time was Detroit). After the flood they picked up the threads again, and began to live the life they had longed for. Everybody took time to relax and enjoy himself. Some wit once said that fun is not where you find it but where you make it – and they made plenty. In the winter, weddings were the great fun-makers. Feasting and dancing began the day before and lasted four or five days – and nights.

In 1830, a breath-taking event took place: a wedding reception for no less a personage than Governor Simpson and his bride. Simpson had gone to England and married his cousin, and the couple had come from Montreal by canoe. The groom was forty-three, the bride seventeen, and no doubt there were snickers and snide remarks. But "even the straight-laced old ladies, after a bit of head-shaking, were agog with excitement," wrote Ross, "and spent weeks making a dress to wear . . . while the lively groom bubbled with happiness." Many years later, Simpson wrote, "As far as good cheer goes, Red River is a perfect Canaan."

The Buffalo Wool Company – and Other Fiascos. Amazing man, George Simpson; he loved his job – producing profits – but he seems to have loved the people too. Of course when the interests of the two clashed, he had to decide in favour of profits. But he must be given credit, even though some historians contend that his motives were suspect, for promoting over a period of some fifteen years no less than seven massive projects intended to im-prove the lot of the settlers. Some of them were quite feasible; but they were all badly executed and all of them failed, most of them ignominiously.

The first was the Buffalo Wool Company. Too many wolves to raise sheep? Then we'll gather buffalo wool! Sounded simple, and profitable, but it wasn't; and the organizers must have been "wool-gathering" not to have realized the many reasons why. And the company was farcically run – into the ground – by all concerned, including Simpson's favourites appointed to the man-agement. Some of the settlers became intoxicated with the scheme, threw down their hoes, and gloated over receiving four dollars a day. Work was neglected until this earliest boom in Manitoba history collapsed like a balloon. The HBC, which had provided the backing, just "forgot" the $25,000 owed it.

Then there was the model farm in St. James. (Actually, over a period of years, there were four such farms.) No expense was spared: buildings, stock – including a $1,500 stallion – "cushy" jobs and a high-salaried manager who shouldn't have switched from furs to farming. This time the trustees of the Selkirk estate paid the shot – nearly $20,000.

Another dream, the Assiniboine Wool Company, fast became a nightmare; it resulted in "much cry and little wool." Then came a project, the Flax and Hemp Company, which especially showed lack of forethought; there was simply no market for flax and hemp. The settlers planted the seed provided and it grew beautifully; but in the fall, having learned the hard facts, they simply left the crop to rot. Then Simpson and his agriculturists apparently decided that sheep could be raised after all. Well-outfitted horsemen made the long trip to Kentucky, bought some 1,500 sheep, started back – and arrived home with 251!

Enter the Red River Tallow Company, which meant raising cattle on a grandly expanded scale. In the first year, wolves, "forty below" weather and deep snow got eighty-five of the cattle, and others also met misfortunes of various kinds. (The settlers had put 473 of their own animals into the scheme.) In the second year, many things, including nature, conspired against the project. But this one was especially Simpson's "baby" and he prodded it on and on till it died – like most of the cattle.

Free Traders Defy the HBC. Whether or not monopoly was entirely to blame for these failures, it was certainly the villain. You couldn't start a store (even Lord Selkirk's had been quickly replaced by a Company store). You couldn't get together with your neighbours to elect representatives to a town council, so you couldn't raise taxes for schools, and so on. The only way to get enough money to buy even an extra Red River cart was by free trading, and that was *verboten*. So the independent types, naturally, became free traders.

Probably none of these men knew that two thousand years ago the Greeks had pointed out an obvious fact: laws not supported by the people cannot be enforced. But they did know that Simpson couldn't build a wall and place sentries all along the border. They did know that as early as 1830, a new and better route had been found to a fur post in Minnesota Territory called Pig Eye's (later St. Peter's, then St. Paul); and that there was a burgeoning American market for buffalo *hides* (used for making belts for machines) and buffalo robes. So it wasn't long before heavily-loaded Red River carts were meeting at midnight, and stealing away southward.

Of course, such leakages eventually threw the London Committee into a tizzy and they ordered their "man," Simpson, to stop that sort of thing. It wasn't cricket! The "Jolly Governor" had to obey, and the result was the darkest chapter in his "reign." His men were sent snooping – invading houses, looking for furs. They searched for hiding places, poked poles up chimneys, opened mail, interrogated – even arrested householders, and put some in chains. All this, in a British country, where "an Englishman's home is his castle!"

HBC officials were so obsessed with plugging holes in the monopoly that they treated their own employees as potential smugglers. When an employee returned to England after years of faithful service, his baggage was searched "lest there be some contraband contained therein." If he was wearing a beaver or martin coat, it was confiscated, even if he claimed that it had been a present from an Indian.

Some of the most successful among the free traders were at once adventurous characters as well as solid, responsible men of business. The best example of this was the man who was the first to become a free trader. He was Andrew McDermot, an Irishman who had come out as a Company servant, served his full seven years' apprenticeship, and then decided he wasn't the "servant type." He became so successful in getting around regulations that Simpson, apparently to save his officers embarrassment, issued him a licence to trade in furs, provided he sold the furs to the Company. Ross says of McDermot that he "could speak the language of the Indians better than the Indians themselves," that he "could run like a deer and endure cold like an Eskimo dog," and that "there was no better judge of men and horses in Red River, nor any man who was his equal in address, humour, shrewdness, and the power of making money." By 1840, he was the richest man west of Lake Superior, and he married one of his daughters to the Governor of Assiniboia. Another daughter became the wife of A.G.B. Bannatyne, who also "graduated" to free trading. Bannatyne did not get the same "preferred" treatment; in fact, the HBC took him to court in England to prevent his "resignation" – and lost. He was too proud to become just a junior partner in his father-in-law's prosperous enterprises, so he started his own. Eventually he was equally admired and respected – and almost as rich.

The Métis hated the Company with its restrictions even more

than the whites did. But most of them also hated the thought of settling down and just farming, which for them would be like living in prison. They were free souls – or free-wheeling spirits – to whom "smuggling" was a meaningless term: "These Americans – they want our furs? So let's take furs to them!" To the Métis, the Company was unfair, and for a special reason: it allowed their "cousins," the Indians, to trade across the border. In many other countries, the natives had revolted against the white man's restrictions, sometimes massacring their oppressors. The Métis were "natives," but only in the sense that they had been born in the country. Ross says, "They are emotional but never violent." And later, historian Alexander Begg wrote that whenever they came in to Fort Garry, "they made their presence known . . . with drinking, gambling, fighting, dancing, laughing, talking, swearing, horse-racing, trading and singing – they made a perfect Babel of the place." But "with all this wildness, we never heard of a case of murder among them."

Some HBC officers also unwittingly helped turn the English-speaking mixed-bloods against the Company. Apparently the snobbishness of one particular officer was chiefly responsible. He was the guardian of the daughter of a distant fellow-officer, and this girl had two suitors, a Scottish lad and an English-speaking mixed-blood, who also happened to be a leader among his people. She preferred the latter, but when she told her guardian he flew into a rage, sent for the girl's "chosen one," and cursed him as a "dirty half-breed" who had no business "aspiring to the hand of a lady accustomed to the first society." From that time, his countrymen "clubbed together in high dudgeon and joined the French Malcontents."

The "Jolly Governor" Tightens the Screws. Simpson did nothing to halt the deteriorating relations; in fact, he himself made a colossal mistake. In 1839, he imported from Montreal a lawyer, Adam Thom, to act as "Recorder" (Judge) for Assiniboia. Thom could not speak French, the language of more than half the people, and worse, he had been a bitter and outspoken enemy of Papineau, the *patriotes'* leader, in the Rebellion of 1837, a fact which the Métis were well aware of. He would have been distrusted anyway, even by the whites, because he was a "Company judge." "Everybody felt sure," says Bryce, "that this 'ogre of justice' had come to uphold the Company's pretensions and to restrict their liberties." He did just that; in fact, some of his decisions were so unfair that the London Committee had to disallow them.

By the mid-1840's, tension was such that a showdown was inevitable. If Simpson was not prepared to recommend to the Committee that the monopoly be given up – and he was not – then he simply had to resort to employing "soldiers to keep the malcontents in line." A drastic step, but he took it, and in 1846 a company of some 350 soldiers arrived. The Committee had to have an excuse of course, so it used the Oregon dispute on the West Coast as its pretext: the Americans had become so belligerent that they might invade Assiniboia! But the joker was that the troops were sent months after the Oregon affair had been resolved.

Stationed at Red River for two years, the soldiers did benefit the settlement in two ways: they spent lots of money, and they sparked a new and exciting social life. The high point was their farewell ball; a letter from Dr. John Bunn to Donald Ross at Norway House says: "Polkas, gallops, waltzes, quadrilles, cotillions, country dances, reels and jigs, employed the heels and talents of the assembly." "At midnight," he wrote, "all became hiccups and happiness!" and "next day brought headaches and recollections." He comments about the reaction to dancing by the clergy: "Had the parsons reserved their fire they could have preserved their character for good sense . . . but they railed at dancing as a damnable sin!" And he adds with a flourish: "Parsons may dispense brimstone but the girls will dance! *Vive la bagatelle!*"

He also stated that "the Misses Caroline Pruden and Margaret and Harriet Sinclair, were, I believe, considered the belles of the evening." In 1923, Harriet (daughter of free-trader James Sinclair) remembered, with a far-away look, that she had worn long white kid gloves, the first seen at Red River; and that she had danced the "daring" polka.

The Showdown. The important effect of Governor Simpson's actions, in turning Red River into what was, in essence, a police state, (even though a fairly mild one) was to goad an element of the people into action. In the late 1840's, a petition was sent to Queen Victoria, another to the British Government, and one to the Legislature of Canada, with the plea to be freed from the throttling grip of monopoly. The British government sent an answer – to Simpson! It supported the HBC's "rights." Perhaps this is what emboldened Simpson to set up his prosecution of free-traders, thus bringing the Profits vs. People battle to a climax in a famous court case.

In the spring of 1849, four Métis, whose leader was William Sayer, were prosecuted for "illegal" trading with Indians. They were arrested and held for a while in the Company jail. They were then released on bail and called for trial on May 17. The Métis were furious, some were tempted to use their guns when the date for the trial was announced: Ascension Day – a Holy Day for Catholics! "We have been persecuted," they cried, "and now our religion is being insulted!"

On the morning of the trial, an estimated 300 Métis gathered in St. Boniface, stacking their guns outside the church. After the service inside they held a meeting at the front. The chief speaker, and apparently their leader, was Louis Riel, Senior, a fiery orator. (His son Louis, five years old at the time, would play a larger, similar role in Manitoba history twenty years later.)

Riel urged immediate release of the prisoners, then asked his aroused listeners to follow him to the courthouse and rescue them if necessary. In this he "obtained a veritable triumph," for they streamed across the river behind him. Confrontation had come, a tense situation for Judge Thom to face: several hundred armed men milling around the courthouse, sensing that history was being made.

When the trial opened, Riel and James Sinclair entered with Sayer, while twenty armed Métis stood guard at the door. Sayer confessed, and a French-English jury found him guilty. But then he stated that a Company Officer had given him authority to trade with Indians. What could Thom do? Like a bully surrounded by his victims, he looked at the hostile faces in the courtroom, squirmed – perhaps some of the Métis felt a touch of pity for him – wavered, and finally piped that he would "withhold sentence." Under the circumstances existing at the time he did not – dared not – put the three men accused with Sayer on trial. All four walked out of the courtroom free men!

Free men! Free *trade* – that's what it meant to the crowd! Outside there was bedlam! French-speaking, English-speaking; Indians, whites, hybrids; hunters, traders, settlers – all shouting *"Le commerce est libre!* The trade is free!"

61

It had finally happened. The monopoly – what some regarded as the tyranny of the Company – had been trampled into the ground. The people had won and were "free." The greatest evidence that the HBC had lost was that Adam Thom, the personification of the monopolistic "profit" system, was demoted to secretary of the court.

CHAPTER 5

"Tolerably Virtuous and Unmistakably Happy" (1850-1860)

In its long history the HBC *had survived the threats to its monopoly from the French and the* NWC, *only to be humbled by a handful of Métis. It still had its vast fur fields in the North; and these it now had to depend on to keep up dividends, because free-traders increased in numbers until, by 1860, their combined trade amounted to nearly half of that of the company itself.*

For the people of Assiniboia, freedom from monopoly made life more pleasant. They suffered one affliction, but only one: a flood that was over in a month or so. In fact, if we compare life in this period with that in any earlier – or later – period, we are disposed to believe the glowing reports of visitors (some called Red River a "Utopia"); and even the nostalgic writings of the people themselves decades later. This, it seems, was their "happy time."

The Battle of the Grand Coteau. After their Sayer court victory, the Métis flexed their muscles, ready to take on any force threatening their beautiful carefree life. The Sioux gave them the opportunity. In the summer hunt of 1851, there was a main party from St. Boniface and a smaller group from Grantown: the two parties travelled parallel courses about thirty miles apart. About five hundred miles southwest of Red River on the Grand Coteau (the watershed between the Assiniboia and the Missouri), the scouts of the Grantown party reported a large concentration of Sioux – later estimated at 2,500 warriors – moving towards them. Quickly, with the military precision learned from Cuthbert Grant, the carts were placed in a circle, wheel to wheel, and the horses and oxen herded into a corral in the enclosure. The women dug pits under the carts in which to shelter their children, while the

hunters – there were only seventy-seven of them, some of them boys as young as twelve – dug rifle pits several yards out in front of the barricade.

They were ready none too soon. The Sioux charged and were driven off; charged again and again, wave after wave, each time leaving more and more warriors and horses on the plains. Of the few horsemen who got past the devastating fire from the pits, one was a picturesque young chief – "so handsome," said Jean Baptiste Falcon (son of the poet) "that my heart revolted at the necessity of killing him."

All through the battle, the priest, Father La Fleche, passed from cart to cart, his crucifix in one hand – and a hatchet in the other – encouraging the defenders, soothing the children, and praying. There were no casualties, except for a few horses and oxen. Most of the Sioux bullets, and all their arrows, fell short of the carts.

Then suddenly the Sioux changed their tactics; they surrounded the camp, got off their horses, and crept forward, sniping – and found themselves being picked off. Now there was a long pause; clearly the proud "Tigers of the Plains" had decided the rifle fire was too hot for them. Sitting on their horses, staring in disbelief at the insignificant little camp, their shame grew, and turned to anger. They charged wildly, whooping and yelling, hoping to stampede the horses and oxen. The result: still more of them joined their wounded or dead comrades in the grass.

At last the sun set, night fell, and men, women, and children, looking up in thankfulness, looked up again in awe – the moon was moving into eclipse. Perhaps to the Sioux it was an evil omen; in fact, one report of the battle says that a chief was heard to cry, "They have a Manitou with them – it is impossible to kill them!" Soon the Indians were loading their wounded into the carts they had brought to carry away the plunder from the Métis camp – and they rode away. Then suddenly from above came a deafening crash – a thunder storm! To Father La Fleche, no doubt, it was a heavenly hosanna; to the imaginative Falcon, perhaps a salute to the victors from the Olympian gods.

The Métis knew the Sioux would be back, but decided to break camp and try to join the main party. Thanks again to Cuthbert Grant's training, they executed their withdrawal brilliantly. The next day the Sioux did attack again; and for five hours the little band went through the same ordeal – with the same results. Then a chief rode up, palm upraised in the recognized gesture of peace. The Sioux, he declared, had had enough; never would they attack the Métis again. Then he left, and as the proud but humiliated warriors rode out of sight – *crash* – another thunder storm!

It had been an amazing victory, the supreme achievement of the Métis "nation." Outnumbered thirty to one, they had lost only one man: a captured scout tried to escape and was cut down – with three bullets and sixty-seven arrows! The Sioux left eighty warriors and sixty-five horses on the field. It was, in fact – like the Sayer trial – an historic victory. The trial had freed the colony from monopoly; this victory freed both the colony and the trade routes southward from the Sioux menace.

Tripping to St. Paul: Three Months of Delight. What this second triumph did for the Métis' pride can be imagined. Who said they were just happy-go-lucky children of the plains! Demean themselves by hiring themselves out as lowly labourers on the white settlers' farms – for 37 cents a day? *Sacre bleu,* they would not! Not as long as they were in demand as *voyageurs,* York boatmen, cart drivers and buffalo hunters.

They were now in more demand than ever, especially for tripping to St. Paul. With the restrictions removed from trading, business with the American post increased by leaps and bounds. Then in 1858 came a development that was little short of sensational. Simpson arranged with the American government for all HBC goods, ingoing and outgoing, to be shipped in bond through the United States. St. Paul had replaced York Factory as the port of entry to Rupert's Land! A shot in the arm, indeed – for both Red River and St. Paul – and the traffic sky-rocketed!

By 1860, there were six thousand carts in the St. Paul "service"; and cart trains were hauling, annually, a quarter of a million dollars' worth of furs and hides – and pemmican, which even some European nations had discovered to be the ideal food for their armies. Profits on the trade, added to that from the cart-families' lavish spending, put a million dollars a year into the pockets of St. Paul's traders and merchants.

And the Métis, out-door and out-going types that they were, loved the long trip southward. Usually they took their families with them despite the jarring, uncomfortable ride, the two-mile-an-hour pace of the oxen, and the unearthly screech of the ungreased wooden axles (grease, impregnated with dust, would have worn out the axles in no time).

The trains were organized on military lines, like the buffalo hunt; and even though they were often a mile or more long, the carts were always wheeled into a circle at night. Ah, night! With sentries posted and all the chores completed, the "children of the plains" really became children – singing, dancing to the fiddle, skylarking – even making love – around the big bonfires. A long trip it was, six weeks or more, but a fun one. And at the end, St. Paul, with all its "American" frontier-town excitement!

And how these "foreigners" fascinated the Americans! One writer described them as "wild, picturesque, with free, firm step; bold, yet graceful abandon of carriage . . . and bronzed features." They wore "blue coats with enormous buttons of polished brass; sashes of brightest red; jaunty little caps; trousers of corduroy . . . and moccasins." And "within their camp is heard a strange mélange of languages, as diverse as their parentage – French, English, Cree, Ojibway – with mingled accent, soft and musical, abrupt and guttural, in strange and startling contrasts."

The 1852 Flood. One April morning in 1852, a tripman, sleeping in his shack in a swampy bend of the Red, awoke to find a frog on his pillow. The river had risen several inches overnight; and it continued to rise until it was within eighteen inches of the 1826 flood level. (Curiously, the date of the crest, May 22, was the same in both floods.) "Houses and barns," wrote one of the settlers, "were floating in all directions like sloops under sail, with dogs and poultry in them. . . . The very mice, snakes and squirrels could not find a safe place." More damage was done than in 1826, because there was now more property. But the new generation showed the never-say-die spirit of their parents and quickly recovered.

One family, the Campbells, escaped much suffering because of their "Grandfather." Long before the water began to rise, this wide-awake oldster "thought he saw signs," like those that had preceded the 1826 disaster, and he informed the "young folks." They paid no attention, but he went into action. On the highest part of his son's land he found a spot between four big trees and, like Noah, began to build. By the time he had the framework of a house up and anchored to the four trees, the river was rising fast. The family, all ten of them, rushed to help, while "Grand-

67

father" chortled to himself. And in half the "normal" time, they had their "ark" plastered and water-proofed, so that it would float – and the family moved in.

The river rose higher and higher. And the house rose too! But it didn't float away. They had stored pemmican in it, and various non-perishable foods. In their dugout canoe they would gather dead trees with dry branches for firewood. They even went to church, tying the canoe to the steps of St. Boniface Cathedral which also was on high ground.

Twelve Families Found Portage La Prairie. In 1826, the farthest settlement west along the Assiniboia was Grantown. By 1852, it was Portage la Prairie, not far from the strategic spot where La Vérendrye had built Fort la Reine. It was founded the year before the flood by twelve families led by the Anglican Archdeacon Cochrane and Peter Garrioch.

These pioneers soon realized that they had, as Garrioch said, "come upon a little Eden." Not only was it an unspoiled, idyllic location, but it provided everything necessary for an easy, though simple, life – without too much work. Hay was to be had for the cutting, wood for the chopping; and many kinds of wild fruit grew in abundance. The river furnished sturgeon, pike and perch; Lake Manitoba, white fish. Wild ducks swarmed in the sloughs, wild pigeons and partridges in the woods. Only a little further west the buffalo herds still roamed; and wolf, fox, lynx, and bear provided fur and sport. (There might even have been grizzly bears; in 1847, the English surveyor, John Palliser, shot two near Turtle Mountain.) And the soil? The Portage plains were to become one of the West's great wheat-growing areas.

But these pioneer farms were not actually on the Portage *plains*; nor were there any farms in all "Manitoba" out on the plains; they were all river lots. The original Selkirk's settlers' lots had by this time been subdivided, some of them two or three times, to create new farms for grown sons. (Visiting Easterners, seeing some as narrow as a hundred yards, referred to them as "farming lanes.") But they were all still river lots, as were the lots in all the new settlements. It would be another thirteen years before a single settlement was established away from the river. The reason? It was simply accepted by everyone that you could not farm on the open prairie – and no one with a family to feed

68

was going to try it. It was to take "ignorant" people who "didn't know any better" to prove this notion a fallacy.

The Village of Winnipeg. Although most of the suburbs of present-day Winnipeg had been established, there was still no Winnipeg until 1862. In that year, at the junction of the two main trails, on the bald prairie surrounded by emptiness, Henry McKenney built a store. And was laughed at. When people saw it, they guffawed – it was too far from anywhere, even from the river, the only source of water. And when they saw its long shape, they laughed again, and jeered, and named it "Noah's Ark"; they told him he could go sailing in it every spring because that spot was low and swampy.

But McKenney was not going to be laughed out of his plans, and before long McDermot was erecting buildings near his. The result was a land boom, Winnipeg's first of many. The price of land went up from $185 an acre to $1,500, and even $2,000. McKenney was right.

The bubble burst, though, and Winnipeg remained a village, simply because settlers did not come, and the people living all around the village still sneered at it. They called it McDermottown because McDermot now owned most of the buildings in it. But the crossroads of the West, Portage and Main, had been determined, and the foundations of the future metropolis had been already laid. And the founding seems to have been different from that of any other city in Canada or the United States in that it started in the centre of a community that, by New World standards, was already old.

A Presbyterian Minister Arrives – Forty Years Late! Throughout these years, the simple, almost peasant life of the original settlers did not change a great deal; the long-throttled spirit of enterprise, released by the Sayer court victory, had affected them little. By 1850, most of them were in their sunset years, and they were happy to go on with their unprogressive farming and their simple pleasures. But the Presbyterians among them, which meant the majority, were still angry at not being sent a minister. And they had been humiliated when their most recent petition came back from York Factory as the cover on a crock of butter.

Then in 1851 came unbelievable news. The Canadian Presbyterian Church was sending them a minister, Rev. John Black.

When he arrived in Kildonan, there was prayerful thanksgiving and rejoicing, and he soon proved to be "a man mighty in the scriptures." One grevious disappointment to the oldest of the old-sters: he did not "have the Gaelic!" (Oddly enough, he did "have" French.) A disappointment to all the rest: he stopped the dancing at weddings – but not for long.

Black had hardly begun his work among his flock when the flood struck. They had all laboriously gathered timber, stone, and lime for the building of a church, only to see most of their material washed away. But even a flood could not stop a Presbyterian minister, especially Rev. Black, from holding church services; and on a spot of high ground he "set up a stone for pulpit" and preached his regular Sunday service. Long years later that stone was built into the church in Kildonan which still bears his name.

After the flood, his people again set about gathering building material. All through the winter, the men, working in teams, dragged stone on sledges from Stony Mountain, and pine from St. Peter's, thirty miles down-river. For two years they worked; and "the sound of axe, hammer, and chisel . . . was music to Kildonan hearts." Everybody "of the faith" contributed money or work, and many gave both. And at last – their own church! It is still standing, and is now known as Old Kildonan Church.

Archdeacon Cochrane: Thundering Preacher. The Anglicans had no such problems, and under Bishop Anderson they steadily expanded their work. Mrs. William Cowan, looking back, said that what she remembered chiefly about the "good Bishop" was that "he preached in lavender kid gloves" and that he "preached too long." One sermon she remembered lasted an hour and a half, and "during the last half hour my husband had a raging tooth-ache."

The Anglicans' Archdeacon Cochrane was an energetic founder of settlements and builder of churches, a stern disciplinarian and a thundering preacher. He not only planned and organized the work of building the stone church at St. Andrew's but did much of the back-breaking work himself. In fact, when some of his parishioners appeared at dawn on the first day of building, hoping to have the honour of turning the first sod, they found Cochrane already there; he had been turning sod for an hour.

To all his "children," Cochrane was like a stern schoolmaster;

and although punishment usually came in the form of a tongue-lashing he did not spare the rod. Once, riding past a teepee, he heard cries from a squaw; so he dismounted, cut a willow stick, and beat the brave who had been beating his wife. And he seems to have been a jack-of-all-trades. If he saw a farmer ploughing a crooked furrow, he would take hold of the plough handles and show him how ploughing should be done. His advice to couples he married was equally down-to-earth. After he had harangued one bride with the usual advice, he said, "Never let your man come to church without his trousers being neatly patched." His most "memorable" sermon was the one he delivered on the Sunday after he had seen his alcoholic hired man fight off imaginary snakes and then drop dead. "He poured and he drank," cried the Archdeacon, almost dancing in his ecclesiastical fervour, "and he danced about like a cock on a red hot griddle!"

Cochrane so loved St. Andrew's Church that he made a simple request: that he be buried within sound of St. Andrew's Rapids. He had his wish, and the manner of his funeral was the highest evidence of the love and admiration his people bore him. Both Presbyterians and Anglicans believed that proper respect could be shown the dead only if the coffin were carried, not on a vehicle, but by mourners – regardless of the distance. This strict rule had been observed after the death of Donald Ross when his body was carried on the shoulders of men, in relays, from near Lower Fort Garry to St. John's churchyard, a distance of eighteen miles. Cochrane was at Portage la Prairie when he died, and, it is said, his body was carried to St. Andrew's – more than seventy miles. He was buried, as he had asked, "within sound of St. Andrew's Rapids."

Women of Courage. There were, of course, many noteworthy women promoting the Christian cause; the wives of some of the missionaries led hazardous – and courageous – lives. Mrs. George McDougall had several terrible experiences when her husband was away from home. Once she fought a smallpox epidemic singlehanded, and lost two of her own daughters. At another time, Indians laid a plot to kidnap all the McDougall children, then got cold feet. She and her husband only heard of the near-tragedy later, from an old chief. And one night she woke up in the middle of the night to find a half-naked drunken Indian at the edge of her bed, staring at her. But he just stared and lurched out the door. Another Mrs. McDougall, the wife of Mrs. McDougall Sr.'s missionary-son, John, found herself in a similar situation – and saved herself by leaping through the scraped wolf-skin that served for a window.

In St. Boniface, Bishop Taché was fortunate in the quality of the Grey Nuns who had come out from Quebec in 1844 and 1850. In the 1920's, Sister St. Laurent remembered her "happy hours" nursing settlers and buffalo hunters and Indians who were down with the smallpox. She told of the daring Sister LaGrave, who painted the walls of the first Cathedral, and who sat on a chair placed on boards "away up high" while the other sisters looked up from below and trembled and prayed for her safety. And of Sister Xavier, who lost an arm in an accident but went on with her work – she even continued to knit and sew. She also told of some of the courageous mothers of St. Boniface, especially Madame Desautels. One day when she was alone with her children, several Sioux appeared at her door and demanded food. They were in an ugly mood and began sharpening their knives and terrorizing the children (perhaps they had been drinking – Indians were generally kind to children). When she gave them all the food she had, they left. And the next day a lone Indian appeared at her door, but this time a sick Indian – sick with smallpox. She took him in, sent her children to the neighbours, and nursed him; stayed with him night and day as long as he lived.

A Nun is Kidnapped – For a Worthy Purpose. In 1855, Sister Ste. Therese, described as "beautiful, tall and fair, vigorous but graceful, selfless and with a certain gentleness," arrived from Quebec. She was assigned to work in Grantown, where, according to the St. Boniface archives, she proved herself "well versed in medicine; in fact, her medical knowledge was astounding and her cures often seemed miraculous." To the Métis of Grantown, she became "our dear Sister doctor."

But after she had been there only three years, news came that shocked and dismayed the community. Sister Ste. Therese and Sister Ste. Marie, with whom she had travelled from the East, had only been on loan to the West and they were ordered back. "The whole Catholic population," according to the archives, "were so moved that they tried to oppose her departure." In St. Boniface, a crowd gathered outside the Cathedral, then went to the convent and pleaded with the Mother Superior. One young mother held up her baby and cried, "Without the *Soeur docteur* I would have lost him!" Nothing could be done; the Sister doctor was under the authority of the East.

But if the women of Grantown were willing to accept defeat, the men were not – not the men who had robbed the Sioux of victory on the Grand Coteau. They laid a plot. First, one of them asked a priest, "What is the penalty for touching a Reverend Sister?" The answer: "Excommunication." Now they knew what to do – and what not to do.

The day of departure came, tearful goodbyes were said, and the caravan left, with the two nuns in Red River carts, but seated in improvised armchairs. It reached the Morris River and was moving along a bush-lined road, when suddenly the air was shattered by fierce yells. The Sioux! Five or six men sprang out of the bushes, whooping like Indians, and rushed to the cart of Sister Ste. Therese, who recognized them at once as men of Grantown. As swiftly and as expertly as if they had rehearsed their parts, they slashed the thongs holding her chair down and lifted it, and her, out of the cart – making sure *to touch only the chair*. They placed her, still in the chair, in a cart they had drawn up, and drove off with their prize, yelling in triumph.

What a joyous homecoming in St. Boniface! So many horsemen and carts appeared from nowhere and joined the triumphant cavalcade that it soon became a long, happy parade. And just as it began to move past the Cathedral, the bells in the "Turrets Twain" rang out for a baptism being performed – but the crowd didn't know that. The bells were ringing to celebrate *her* return home!

The incident was so moving that it won Sister Ste. Therese permanently for Red River. And she lived to found both St. Boniface Hospital and St. Mary's Academy.

The Bells of St. Boniface. The three bells that seemed to be ringing for Sister Ste. Therese had had a strange history. Ordered by Bishop Provencher, they were cast in London by the founders of the Big Ben chimes. When they arrived in York Factory, the York boatmen hired to transport them the seven hundred miles to St. Boniface went on strike – the bells weighed 1,600 pounds. But Andrew McDermot, who could persuade anybody to do anything, got together a crew that took up the challenge – and "delivered the goods." And, on All Saints Day, 1840, the three-toned chimes rang out, to the joy of Bishop Provencher, the people of St. Boniface – and all those with any soul, regardless of race or religion, throughout the settlements.

The bells were to become famous throughout the world. When Rev. John Black journeyed to Red River, his travelling companion was Wesley Bond of Philadelphia and the sound of the bells made such an impression on Bond that he talked and wrote of them back home. It is believed that his story inspired the poet Whittier to write the poem which told of:

> The bells of the Roman Mission
> That call from their turrets twain.

But in 1860, more trouble; the Cathedral caught fire and turrets and bells crashed to earth. Sorrowfully, Bishop Taché, who had succeeded Bishop Provencher, dug into the ruins and found the bells – broken and partly melted. But he salvaged a thousand pounds of metal and sent it back to London via Hudson Bay to be recast.

Then, when the new bells were finished, somebody in London made a mistake and sent them back by way of the United States. They came, by railway, only as far as Duluth. They might as well have been held in London; to bring them the rest of the way by oxcart would have been expensive, and perhaps impossible. So back to London they went again! Eventually they landed at York Factory, having crossed the Atlantic five times! Apparently they were forgotten there for years, and they didn't arrive "home" until 1864.

But still they were not allowed to ring, because Bishop Taché decided that the debts they had incurred must be paid off first. The debts were paid off shortly; everybody, it seems – Catholic and Protestant, rich and poor – sent in money. And once again the bells rang out,

> To the boatman on the river
> To the hunter on the plain.

An Isolated But Contented Community. In the 1850's and 1860's, people produced or made practically everything they used. Every family had its spinning wheel and weaving loom, and each member had his regular jobs, although Mother was the chief "manufacturer." She even made the family's shoes and moccasins, using buffalo sinew as thread. This product of the hunt was

74

indispensable. It came ready-made, coarse or thin, and had many uses. In fact, it was so valuable that for many years it had been the chief item of barter.

Every man built his own house, of course, with logs banked with earth for warmth. Houses were generally heated by one or more Carron stoves, each protruding through a wall to heat two rooms at once. Wealthy families had very large houses; "Sandy" Logan's had twelve rooms, heated by seven Carron stoves, the one in the kitchen with an oven large enough to roast a small pig. Naturally, families provided most of their own food, and mothers learned how to make tempting dishes from staple ingredients; for example, two appetizing soups, Rowschow and Rubaboo, were made from pemmican. Sometimes, they enjoyed items that would be delicacies in any age in any country: buffalo tongue, moose nose, and beaver tail. But tropical fruit was unknown. When a teacher explained to her pupils that the earth was round like an orange, they asked what an orange was like. Drinking water was a health hazard and was always boiled before being used; it came from the river and was peddled from door to door by oxcart.

For many years most families "made do" without two seemingly indispensable items. One was sugar – so no cakes or pies! Those who lived close enough to a stand of maples could have maple sugar, which for the sweet-toothed would help make life more bearable. The other item was salt, so meat could be preserved only by drying. That is, until Joe Monkman appeared on the scene. There were many saline springs, especially in the north, and fur traders at posts not too distant from them had been making salt for some time. Joe established a plant at Salt Springs on Lake Winnipegosis, and for many years peddled his precious product from door to door throughout the widespread settlements.

Food for livestock during the long winter months had to be put up each year, so an annual family project was cutting hay in the "hay privilege" at the end of each river lot, or far out on the prairie. Hay was so important that a man who carelessly set a prairie fire, as sometimes a renegade Indian did for revenge, was regarded as virtually a criminal. There were certain hay-cutting regulations: to give every family a fair chance, a starting date was fixed. Before that date, every enterprising farmer would try to spy out the best hay meadow, and pre-empt his hay-area by cutting a swath around it with his scythe. In dry years, the farmers could not take any chances, so they would go out the night before the starting day and be ready to start cutting on the stroke of midnight, even in the middle of a thunder storm. And during the weeks of haying they camped out, riding home only on Saturday nights. All of which does not mean that they were greedy: when a prairie fire destroyed the hapstack of one of the MacBeths, his neighbours dumped a hundred cart-loads of hay in his farmyard.

Red River's aristocracy existed on a somewhat different scale. It was made up chiefly of retired HBC men, some with Indian or halfbreed wives. In their large, handsome stone houses, most of them at St. Andrew's (the "Tuxedo" of the time) lived like English squires. Their houses were likely to be richly furnished, with much of the contents imported from England. Visitors to Red River were naturally surprised to find people living so graciously "on the frontier."

By 1846 some of these "solid citizens" even had spotted English coach dogs to follow their English carriages. One, John Peter Pruden, a retired HBC officer, lived up-river on Lot 13 with an English wife near St. John's Cathedral. He possessed a tamed wild goose, which would half waddle and half fly beside the dog. Every fall for several years it joined geese flying south, returning in the spring.

One of the great advantages of living along the river was that houses were not far apart. Red Riverites never knew the loneliness which in later years bore with such crushing weight upon the pioneers, especially the women, out on the bare prairie. There was always "something going on": parties (one of the popular games was a hugging match), concerts, and weddings.

A wedding was always a great event. It was the custom to hold it on a Thursday before noon, and then there would be several days of merrymaking and dancing. On Sunday, the newly-wedded couple would drive to church for the "kirking"; and if it was wintertime, their friends, in their sleighs behind the fastest horses their fathers could afford, would – if their fathers weren't watching – "profane the Sabbath" by racing to church. One rule: you were never to pass the newlyweds. The bride would not be taken to her husband's house until Tuesday; and the merry-making would go on – presumably without the newlyweds – until sunrise Wednesday.

New Year's Day, rather than Christmas, was the great annual festival. It was ushered in by much firing of guns, and the men (not the women) went about making calls. And so did the Indians, in full war paint; they would "dance for their supper." They would be given, said one lady, "little cakes with currants in them – which mustn't be left out," and tea, which they loved more than tobacco – but not as much as liquor.

The Métis seem to have enjoyed themselves whatever they were doing, but dancing was almost an obsession with them. A writer of the times says that "these men who ran with the dog carrioles in winter and were boatmen in summer could run or row all day and then dance all night." A group of traders at Fort Garry gave a demonstration of this. To settle an argument as to how far Headingly was, they asked a Métis, with a pedometer attached to his capote, to run there and back. He agreed, and ran the distance; when he handed back the pedometer next morning, it registered not twenty, buy seventy-seven miles! There had been a dance at Headingly.

A correspondent for an American magazine who had attended a Métis dance wrote: "Jigs, reels and quadrilles were danced in rapid succession . . . a black-eyed beauty and a strapping *Bois Brulé* would jump up from the floor and outdo their predecessors in figure and velocity, the lights and shadows chasing each other faster and faster over the rafters. . . . And above the loud laughter rose the monomaniac fiddle-shrieks of the trembling strings, as if a devil was at the bow."

An intriguing feature of Red River was the complex of languages spoken. The American, J.W. Taylor, wrote that, on four successive Sundays, he heard sermons in five different languages: in St. Boniface, Latin and French; in St. Peter's, Cree (by a full-blooded Indian clergyman); in Kildonan, Gaelic; and in St. John's, English. If he had tried to engage the Indians at St. Peter's in conversation, he might have also discovered a commonly used dialect, Bungi (variously spelled Bungay, Bungee, even Bangie). It was an "exquisite composite jargon, "said one writer, and it contained words and expressions from English, French, Gaelic, Cree, and other Indian languages. It had been evolving, it seems, for a century or more; and it can still be heard in the "down-river" area and along some of the trade routes. To some who have heard it, Bungi sounds like Pidgin English. Another visitor wrote that "the Indians speak English with a Scotch accent."

Clearly, Red River was a pleasant place to live. Alexander Begg, looking back in 1879, wrote:

> We had no bank, no insurance office, no lawyers, only one doctor, no City Council, only one policeman, no taxes — nothing but freedom; and though lacking several other so-called advantages of civilization, we were, to say the least, tolerably virtuous and unmistakably happy. Mr. James Mulligan was the last policeman under Hudson's Bay Company sway and that gentleman may remember how on one occasion a few fun-loving individuals . . . took him, bound him to a cart, and deposited him in the jail, much to his astonishment. He took the joke very good-naturedly.

Very good-naturedly! That seems to symbolize the attitude of the Red Riverites of the time.

CHAPTER 6

The Riel Resistance
and the Creation
of the Province (1860-1870)

By 1860, Red River was becoming less of an island in a fur-trade ocean. Many developments were making it, so to speak, part of the "mainland," the outside world: trade with St. Paul, improved mail service, steamboats on the Red, and a newspaper.

Then, in 1867, four Canadian provinces in the East formed the Dominion of Canada, and a clause in the British North America Act provided for the acquisition of Rupert's Land. Young Canadians had been seeking homesteads in the American West; Canada needed a "West" of its own. And at last an agreement was reached by which, on December 1, 1869, Rupert's Land was to become a part of the Dominion.

Many stormy events were to intervene. The chief trouble was the uncertainty surrounding the transfer of the land. Why had the inhabitants not been consulted? What would be the status of Red River in the Dominion? Would the inhabitants have their property rights safeguarded? The Métis' fears were intensified when, a year before the completion of the bargain, the government of Canada sent surveyors into the territory. Some of these men acted in a high-handed manner, driving in stakes and running their lines across private lands, climbing over fences, tramping through crops, and boasting that the Métis would soon be put in their place. It is not surprising that they decided to resist; and they found an able leader in young Louis Riel.

Ross House. In 1855 came an event that to the older settlers was sensational: a post office, the first between the Great Lakes and the Rockies, was opened at Red River. William Ross, son of the historian, was appointed postmaster, and the post office was in

79

his own house on James Street. It continued to serve the settlements along the rivers for many years; then a regular post office was built and the original one was forgotten by most people for three-quarters of a century.

It was not forgotten by the Manitoba Historical Society; and when in 1949 the Ross property was required for a new warehouse, the Society's officers persuaded the City to save the house. With the co-operation of the City, the Province and the CPR they were able to have it moved to a lot in Sir William Whyte Park opposite the CPR Station. It was given the name "Ross House," and restored inside and out. Today, visitors can see many household articles of Ross's time: an organ, oil lamps, a spinning wheel, photograph albums, hand-made chairs, a Carron stove, brass kettles, candle moulds, muskets and swords, and a ladder stairway on pulleys which can be raised and lowered. Letters and cards may still be mailed from the house. A special cachet is used, indicating that the mail has been posted at Manitoba's first post office.

Steamboat 'Round the Bend. Red River, with its trade southward, had "made" St. Paul, or at least enabled it to put down roots; and in 1859, St. Paul, in a sense, "made" Red River. The Minnesota town's merchants realized that a new kind of transportation was needed to supplement the creaking cart brigades, so they offered a bounty for the construction of a steamboat on the Red. And Captain Anson Northup dismantled his ramshackle, paddle-wheel, Mississippi boat (which looked like a raft with a top-heavy superstructure), hauled her on sleighs 150 miles from the Crow Wing River to the Red, put her together again, and set her chugging northward. He and his few passengers should have taken out extra life insurance before going aboard: her ancient locomotive engine shot a continuous fireworks display of sparks into the air – and she was carrying a hundred kegs of gun powder!

But this Rube Goldberg contraption, eating up nearly a cord of wood an hour, panted on 'round the bends – so many bends were there that from Georgetown to Fort Garry was twice the distance a crow would fly. But after eight days (the passengers living on borrowed time), a little girl playing on the walk-way on Fort Garry's walls heard something strange, and said, "Somebody's blowing on a bottle." Every Indian along the river had

been terrified at the sight and sound of the thing. Farmers were dumbfounded, and rushing down to the river they shouted, wept, prayed and shot off their muskets. When the apparition wheezed its way to the Forks, the soldiers in the fort fired a salute and the St. Boniface bells rang. Everybody not out on the summer buffalo hunt tore down to the bank of the river, waving and shouting, and crowded close to see if it was real. Even some Indians whooped, said a report – not realizing that now their way of life was doomed. An historic, if somewhat comic, voyage, it did not just supplement the Red River cart; it heralded its passing. The HBC got the message and put up $20,000 for a "monster" steamer, the *International*. On its first trip north, it carried two hundred passengers – 160 of them, incidentally, Canadians bent on reaching the Caribou gold strike. They got a vivid picture of life – animal life – on the prairies. Their ship was tied to a tree for a whole day while a solid mass of buffalo crossed the river.

Ownership of the *International* gave the HBC another monopoly. For a few years it was the only steamship on the river (the *Anson Northup* had wheezed its last), so the Company could set freight rates. That is, it could until a young Ontario tinsmith, Jimmie Ashdown, persuaded the other merchants in the village to sign up for shares in, of all things, a new steamer. (Jim Ashdown, his grandson, still has the handwritten contract he drew up.) They got her built and, amid loud huzzahs from the whole business community, which meant a dozen or so men, sent her off on her maiden voyage – only to have her rammed and sunk, "accidentally," by the *International*. But they got her floated, back in business and paid for in one summer. Freight rates did come down – but not by much.

The *Anson Northup*, before being crushed by ice at its mooring in the spring of 1862, had helped make a bit of agricultural history. Forty-two years earlier, a handful of Selkirk settlers had made a great trip south on snowshoes to Prairie du Chien on the Mississippi and brought back boatloads of seed wheat. In 1860, the *Anson Northup* carried four sacks of seed wheat from Red River consigned to Prairie du Chien. That little shipment marked the beginning of the exporting of grain from the Canadian prairies.

Manitoba's First Newspaper: the Nor'Wester. In 1859, James Buckingham and William Coldwell, two young Englishmen, decided to start a newspaper in the "Wild West." In St. Paul, they bought a printing plant – one that had seen better days: it had gone through a fire and been patched up by a blacksmith. They loaded it, along with type, paper and ink, into oxcarts and started north. But what a start! The oxen ran away and dumped the type into the street. They gathered it up and went on, but soon found that they were as green at handling oxen as cart drivers would have been at editing a newspaper; it was a month-long nightmare. But somehow they made it, and they set up shop in a log building near Portage and Main. In December, 1859, the *Nor'Wester* made its bow.

They had become monopolists too, of course; there was no other paper between the Great Lakes and the Rockies. But their editorial policy soon ensured them plenty of popular opposition. They argued strongly and persuasively that the country could not remain isolated; that in the new industrial age, government by a fur company was an anachronism. That didn't mean, they said, that Red Riverites should listen to the Americans in their midst who talked of annexing the territory; the "Manifest Destiny" of Red River lay with Canada.

The "Loyal Canadian Party." In the Rebellions of 1837-38, Canadians in both Upper and Lower Canada had fought to throw off monopolistic control of their lives by the Family Compact; and final victory had been won only in 1849 – the very year the people of Assiniboia had thrown off the HBC monopoly. Yet many of the Canadians from Upper Canada who came to Assiniboia only a dozen or so years later seem to have been as arrogant and intolerant as they had accused the Compact of being. They believed, sincerely, that the Northwest *belonged* to Canada, and that, as the prairies would soon be peopled with Canadian settlers, the Métis should not be allowed to stand in the way of "progress."

There were many examples of callous treatment of the Métis. When, for instance, a Métis family in the Headingly district was hunting outside the little piece of land they lived on (squatter's rights had always been recognized), a family of Canadians moved in and refused to move out; and the Council of Assiniboia, to avoid "trouble," did nothing. One of the Canadians working on the Dawson Road, Charles Mair – a well-known poet, strangely enough – so insulted the Métis that he was horsewhipped out of the post office by Mrs. A.G.B. Bannatyne. Some Canadians were quoted as saying, "The half-breeds will be driven out, or kept as cart drivers," and that the coming of the Canadians was "like the march of the sun – it cannot be stopped." So naturally the cry swept the Métis settlements: "They have come to steal our homes!"

In 1860, Dr. John Schultz, a red-headed giant of a man, arrived from Ontario. R.G. MacBeth, a boy at the time, says that one night, to cow a crowd at a meeting, Schultz "put his foot on the bar of a big oaken chair . . . wrenched it asunder as if it had been made of pipe stems." He similarly "wrenched" the peaceful life of the community for several years. Crafty of eye and mind, he set about making money soon after he arrived from Ontario. (He did some doctoring but was said to have had no medical degree.) He spent much of his time agitating against the HBC and leading the "Loyal Canadian Party." In 1865 he bought the *Nor'Wester,* and immediately it became a propaganda sheet for the Canadian "cause."

Schultz and his followers were not entirely to blame for the troubles. By the early 1860's, it had become clear to all that the HBC could not cope with the rapidly changing conditions; there had to be, eventually, a government that could maintain law and order. To the credit of the Canadians, they did realise this. In fact, at a meeting in St. James, one of them called for the formation of a provisional government.

Archdeacon Cochrane had set up a local government for the little settlement at Portage la Prairie and it had provided good service; but it died with him in 1865.

The Republic of "Manitobah." In 1867, Thomas Spence, an "odd ball" if there ever was one, moved to Portage la Prairie from Red River and set about persuading the Portage people to let him organize a republic. A republic within the British Empire! Surprisingly, they did. Borrowing the name of the nearby lake, he called it the "Republic of Manitobah." Thomas Spence, being the Father of his Country, became its President, just as George Washington had in his. And in a few months he had government machinery set up and operating.

But soon a fly appeared in the ointment, in the person of McPherson, the shoemaker. Instead of sticking to his stitching, McPherson went about the settlement telling people that the money they paid in taxes to the new Republic was being spent on whiskey for the President and his cronies. What could a poor President do but bring the force of the law against this slanderer? McPherson was indicted for treason and a warrant issued for his arrest. The state's entire police force – two constables, Hudson and Anderson – were dispatched to bring the accused in – "dead or alive." This being dangerous work – and cold – (it was the middle of winter) the two minions of the law first fortified themselves with government whiskey. Then they set forth in their government sleigh, its bells tinkling merrily and the constables bellowing their mission against "this here law breaker."

When they came to McPherson's cobbling shop they entered valiantly and said their piece. Then they engaged in a little friendly wrestling with their quarry – two against one! Soon McPherson dashed out, presumably leaving the two wrestling each other, ran wildly, and got stuck in a snowbank. The lawmen rode up in comfort and somehow got him into the sleigh, although almost minus his pants.

The villain of the piece had now become the victim, so a hero was needed. And if, as some wit has said, "Time is that which heroes have the knack of arriving in the knick of," then John McLean is our hero. A stern-faced patriarch of Portage and a legendary battler for the rights of man, McLean was on his way home when the sleigh drew up. McPherson leaped out, holding up his tattered pants, and ran to him, crying, "Save me!" The constables tore after him, but McLean placed himself, like a Colossus, between them and the pursued and shouted, "Stand back!" That sobered the constables somewhat and they explained the situation. McLean, to McPherson's disappointment, advised him to go peacefully; but swore that he would be present at his trial. McPherson went off with the lawmen.

The trial was held that night in Hudson's house, and McLean appeared, accompanied by three miners who were visiting at his home. As well as the two constables and a brother of one of them, Spence was there, sitting as judge at the end of a long table with a lamp on it. The accused, McPherson, sat at the other end. The Republic's hour of trial had come.

Things proceeded in fairly orderly fashion, but only until McLean asked who was the accuser in the case. When Hudson said that Spence was, McLean exploded. "Come oot o'that y'whited sepulchre! Y'canna act as judge and accuser baith!"

That started the brawl rolling; it was a fair fight – four against four. And each knew who he was socking or aiming at – until the lamp got knocked over. After that, it was just a matter of swinging and hoping. Then, in the dark, the miners drew their revolvers and fired into the ceiling. There was sudden silence. From under the table came the plaintive voice of Spence, President of the Republic of Manitobah: "For God's sake men, don't shoot! I have a wife and family!"

As Frank Walker, telling the story in the *Beaver*, comments: "Less poignant phrases have marked the end of states!" This, of course, marked the end of the Republic of "Manitobah."

Louis Riel. Early in life Louis Riel studied to be a priest and he spent seven years at the College de Montreal. But he left the seminary, apparently by mutual agreement, and then worked for three years at various jobs. In 1868, at the age of twenty-four, he returned to Red River, and although he was only one-eighth Indian he became, like his father before him, the leader of the Métis.

The first test of his leadership came in October, 1869: what to do about the Canadian government surveyors? At the head of a party of eighteen unarmed Métis, he rode to the farm in St. Vital where the government men were working and calmly told them that they could not proceed. To reinforce his point, he stood on the survey chain. And the surveying stopped. The second test involved a tale as weird and wonderful in its way as that of Thomas Spence.

"Lieutenant Governor" MacDougall. That fall, William MacDougall, a Minister in Sir John A. Macdonald's government and a Father of Confederation, came West to take over from the HBC as the legally appointed Lieutenant Governor of the Dominion's new territory, arriving almost two months before the day, December 1, the transfer was to be signed.

From Ottawa through the States, he travelled in style. On his staff were aides and innumerable servants; and there were sixty wagonloads of luggage, including furniture for the Lieutenant Governor's suite – plus three hundred Enfield rifles! The farmers in Minnesota must have gawked; at least in cost, the thing compared favourably with the equipage that Queen Victoria might have taken on a Royal Tour of India – there was everything but elephants. This was his second mistake – the first was in coming before he was welcome – and he soon made a third.

The Métis, having organized a National Committee, sent a letter (in French – one of Canada's two official languages) to Pembina to await his arrival, ordering him not to attempt to enter Assiniboia without permission of its people; and to stress the point, they built a *barrière* across the road at St. Norbert. MacDougall hesitated. Then, like a boy thrusting one toe in the water to test the temperature, he crossed the border – just barely crossed it – to the HBC post opposite Pembina. No guns went off, so he ordered an aide, Captain Cameron, to take a detachment and ride to Red River, just to see if they would get there. They did not; they were blocked by the Métis barricade. Cameron, confronted with it, exploded: "Remove that *blahsted* fence!" This brought only French chuckles to the funny English accent. He and his men found their horses being politely but firmly turned around to face south, and in which direction they proceeded. Across the border, MacDougall's horses had been turned around too; he was back at Pembina.

When December 1 dawned, the day that Queen Victoria was to proclaim the "great real estate deal," there was not even a post card from her saying, "So sorry!" (Canada had requested a postponement.) So there was MacDougall, stranded and forlorn in a foreign country, instead of being carried in triumph to his capital, as a Toronto paper actually reported he had been.

Reflecting on his predicament, with no instructions from Ottawa, MacDougall thought up a possible way out of the impasse. No proclamation from the Queen? Very well, he'd issue one himself – in the *name* of the Queen! He again crossed just over the border – after dark, in a howling blizzard – and, with one aide holding up a lantern and another a flag, he cleared his throat and read his improvised "proclamation." There were not even snowbirds present. But when the amazing news reached the East, old ladies tittered, John A. *et al* smiled weakly – and Quebec guffawed. As for the reaction of the Queen herself, when she was duly apprized, it was perhaps at this time that she coined her famous line, "We are not amused."

Writer MacBeth reports that if Riel and his lieutenants had decided the proclamation was genuine, they would have had their men *escort* MacDougall to Fort Garry as they were not rebelling against the Queen. They decided it wasn't.

MacDougall blundered on. He actually ordered Colonel Dennis, his "Conservator of the Peace," to prepare for war: to raise a fighting force for the purpose of putting down an apparent rebellion. Dennis did begin to raise a force, getting the active support of Schultz's Canadians. And he callously recruited Indians – had them drilling with his white recruits. There were even rumours that George Racquette, a notorious scoundrel and agent of Schultz, was inciting the Sioux at Portage.

These actions, of course, accomplished several things, all negative. First, it gave the English settlers the opportunity to issue a statement clarifying their position: "We have not been consulted. . . . The character of the new government has been settled in Canada. . . . When you present to us the issue of a conflict with the French party, with whom we have hitherto lived in friendship . . . feel disinclined to enter upon it, and think that the Dominion should assume the responsibility of establishing among us what it, and it alone, has decided upon." Secondly, it gave Dennis a chance to shout that the settlers were all cowards – which in view of their record of courage was simply funny. As for Riel, it accomplished what he had been unable to do himself: rally the hesitant among the Métis to his side – they no longer doubted the necessity of being organized to defend their homes.

Now the situation was explosive. On November 2, Riel and his men had already taken over the Upper Fort without approval, and Dennis was drilling at the Lower Fort. Strong, non-partisan community leaders, like Bishop Machray and A.G.B. Bannatyne, could not influence Riel; but they could influence Dennis, and they condemned him for equating his partisan cause with loyalty to the Empire – his "Rally 'Round the Flag" call to arms. They convinced him that his confrontation would result only in tragedy. To his credit he ordered his forces disbanded.

Meanwhile, MacDougall was just sitting at Pembina, although he was doing some practice shooting – perhaps a pathetic effort to show that he wasn't to be made a fool of. But with Dennis's failure he realized that he could not accomplish anything by staying there. Finally receiving delayed word from Ottawa (some say deliberately held back before reaching Pembina), he recalled Dennis, who was no longer a menace, and having read the Toronto papers (which among other things called his "invasion" a "most wonderful failure"), he and his entourage started their trek southward through the snow. It was like Napoleon's retreat from Moscow, except that the Métis gave him a send-off: a *chanson* composed by old Pierre Falcon, and sung to the tune of "The Wandering Jew."

"Schultz's Last Stand" or "Who Gets The Government Pork And Beans?" The MacDougall comedy was followed by the Schultz melodrama. According to Peter McArthur, one of Schultz's followers, twenty tons of pork and beans intended for the surveyors and the men building the Dawson Road had been stored in Schultz's warehouse (Main and Water Streets); and Schultz persuaded fifty or sixty of his "Friends of Canada" to establish themselves there to keep Riel from getting it. Cooler heads disapproved of the venture. Bishop Machray and a delegation from the village of Winnipeg tried to convince him that garrisoning men so close to the fort was like waving a red flag at Riel. And one of his own supporters, Dr. O'Donnell, wrote later that "had they gone about their usual business, they would never have been attacked." McArthur, looking back many years later, went even further. He declared that if some of the food had been given to the buffalo hunters – the hunt had failed that year – "there would have been no rebellion."

Riel's men surrounded the warehouse, pointed a loaded cannon at the door, persuaded them to surrender, and marched them off as prisoners to Fort Garry: Schultz spent Christmas Day in solitary confinement. One blizzardly night a month later he escaped: he had somehow made a rope of buffalo hide and had let himself down from his cell. Riel's mounted scouts were under orders to shoot him on sight, but he eluded them. He made his way to Ontario, where he set about appealing to Protestant prejudices. "We must act – or we'll have Quebec popery in power in the West too!" he told Ontario audiences. He had hardly begun his rabble-rousing when the news arrived of the execution of Thomas Scott. After that he didn't need to do anything. Red River had produced a witch's brew; now he could relax and just let it cook.

It did. And Schultz became a hero – in Ontario. And he was eventually rewarded handsomely for his handiwork by the Canadian government. First, it paid him a nice round sum for his "rebellion losses," presumably the pork and other trade goods that went to the fort. Later it made him a Senator; then it appointed him Lieutenant Governor of his "adopted" province. And as a final honour, he was knighted "for services to the Empire."

Smith and Riel Bring English and French Together. After MacDougall's failure, Sir John A. Macdonald at last saw that he would have to send out a mediator, a reconciler of differences. He chose a fellow Scot, Donald A. Smith (the later famous and fabulously rich Lord Strathcona). The two were long associated – and didn't always hit it off. Once in the House of Commons, Sir John said, "That fellow Smith is the damnedest liar I ever met!" And another time: "I could lick him quicker than hell could scorch a feather!"

Donald A. had spent twenty years with the HBC in Labrador. He arrived at Red River in 1869, two days after Christmas, and Riel kept him virtually a prisoner in the fort for three weeks, although the Métis leader allowed him to see people. And it seems that Smith simply "went to work" on some of them, especially the Métis among them. Bribery was accepted, or at least condoned, in public life in those days, and Donald A., like John A., was an old hand at probing to find the "right people" to work on. Realizing at once that not all the Métis were strongly behind Riel, he apparently tried to "divide and conquer" by "crossing the palm" of some of them. Historian Russenholt sees some evidence, in fact, that he spent $12,500 in "greasing" the way for a split in the Métis ranks; and that some of the Red Riverites believed that Smith even "reached for the top." He tried to bribe Riel, and failed; and hated him everlastingly for it.

Earlier, Riel had succeeded in bringing English and French together in a convention and he seems to have been close to persuading them to accept a provisional government – when, on December 1, Dennis arrived from Pembina with copies of MacDougall's "proclamation." No one knew for sure that it was phony and the English decided to wait and see. Now, six weeks later, Smith called a meeting to try to bring the two sides together.

There was no large hall at Red River, so (on January 19, 1870) a thousand men (no women), representing all the parishes along the rivers, assembled in the yard of the fort – with the temperature at twenty below zero. (At that time Schultz was still in the fort.) They listened and asked questions for five solid hours, Riel acting as interpreter; they even came back the next day for more. And at the end of the ordeal they shamed the bigoted on both sides: they agreed that twenty English and twenty French representatives should be elected to meet in a week. It was a great victory for common sense. Said Riel: "I came with fear. . . we are not enemies – but we came very near being so." And Alexander Begg, who was there, wrote: "The utmost good feeling prevailed. French and English shook hands . . . and a spirit of unity appeared."

The upshot was that within a few weeks, English and French, acting together, succeeded in hammering out a mutually acceptable Bill of Rights. Then Smith brought joy to both sides by inviting them to elect delegates, English and French, to go to Ottawa to negotiate. This was a breakthrough; and the English, in turn, overjoyed Riel by agreeing that, in the meantime, a provisional government should be set up with himself as President. And to top it off, Riel removed a great sore spot by promising that the Canadians he was still holding in the fort would be released.

The Shooting of Scott: A Crime – and a Blunder. That night French and English set off fireworks around huge bonfires; but they celebrated too soon. At Portage la Prairie, still a centre of Canadian feeling, plans had been laid to release the prisoners by force. In fact, on the day of the celebrations, some sixty Portage men, (mostly surveyors), led by Major Boulton, were marching towards Fort Garry. (Riel had several hundred men!)

When they reached Headingly, they learned that the prisoners were being released. They knew of the compromise solution arrived at; yet, incredibly, they sent a "loyal" Métis, Gaddy, to urge the other Métis in his splinter group to attack the *homes* of followers of Riel, so as to draw the heads of those homes away from Fort Garry. They marched on, to Kildonan; and there they joined some three hundred like-minded men. One group, made up partly of whites and partly of Indians, was led by Schultz, who had not yet set out on his Ontario crusade. They were dragging a cannon, and singing a song the last line of which was: "For we'll take the fort this morning."

The gathering of this clan of avengers resulted in the first bloodshed. A young Métis labourer, Norbert Parisien, having been captured as a suspected spy, escaped, with a gun. Running wildly from his pursuers, he met a young Kildonan Scot, John Hugh Sutherland, and shot him. John Hugh died the next morning, as did Parisien later, possibly from the blows of the axe used in his recapture.* This double-slaying was made more poignant by the nobility of feeling expressed by the Scottish lad on his deathbed. "He begged earnestly," said his sister, Mrs. Black, "that Parisien should not be punished."

Apparently the tragedy, and John Hugh's words, had a sobering effect on the avengers; the Portage men decided to go home. But revenge seems to have been replaced by bravado or rashness or even stupidity. Realizing that their war-like actions had inflamed Riel and his men once more, they should have travelled singly or in small groups, and given the fort a wide berth. Instead they went in a body and passed close to it. As they should have expected, a party of Métis rode out and arrested some fifty of them, among them Boulton.

Boulton was tried by the "court-martial" procedure of the Métis military organization and condemned to death. Smith and others pleaded for his life but to no avail. But then, only a few hours before he was to be shot, John Hugh's mother went to Riel. Mrs. Black's daughter recalled: "Riel said, 'No . . . I hold him accountable for the death of your son . . . of a man born on the soil of this country.' My mother besought Riel on her knees to give her Major Boulton's life. Riel stopped his pacing up and down, and resting against the end of the table, covered his face with his hands. At last he said, 'Mrs. Sutherland, that alone has saved him. I give you Boulton's life!' "

Then came the tragic event that wise policy on the part of the Canadian government could have avoided: the shooting of Thomas Scott, after a similar trial. Scott, who had first come out to work as a labourer on the Dawson Road, had been imprisoned with Schultz's "pork" party and had attracted Riel's attention by his defiance and abusive language. As Pierre Berton says in *The National Dream*, Scott was a "bigoted Protestant Irishman, totally unyielding, always inflammatory, who was nourished by his own hatreds." He had escaped from the fort, joined the Portage party, and was arrested along with Boulton and the others.

During his second imprisonment he was even more contemptuous of the "inferior" Métis than before (he even tried, according to Berton, to murder Riel). It is possible that Riel would have reprieved him, like Boulton, but his men insisted that the sentence be carried out; Riel didn't dare jeopardize his position

(*Parisien is reported to have recovered)

as leader by relenting. The underlying reason for the shooting, of course, was the affront to the Métis' sensitive yet justifiable pride contained in Scott's viciously expressed contempt for them – the contempt which lay at the root of the trouble the Ontario men raised for themselves.

The shooting was not only a crime but a blunder. Riel had won his case, and peace, though a shocked peace, had returned to Red River. For the Métis leader himself it was a tragedy. "For Riel thereafter," says Morton, "there was no peace in the Northwest he loved, no peace anywhere but the forlorn peace of exile and the final peace of the gibbet at Regina." The incident was to have a tragic, long-lasting effect on Canada. Only three years before, English Protestant and French Catholic had buried their differences in Confederation. Now the old wounds were torn wide open again.

Provincial Status: A Métis Victory. In Ontario, the shock was so great that the three delegates chosen to negotiate with Ottawa had to be brave men to go East at all. But they went, and sure enough, Scott's brother swore out a warrant and had two of them arrested. They were soon released, and in the negotiations that followed they proved courageous – and admirably stubborn. And they won *provincial* status for their homeland! Manitoba would not be a mere part of the vast Northwest Territory run from Ottawa. The Bill of Rights, the chief clause of which demanded self-government, was incorporated in the Manitoba Act, passed May 12, 1870. However, the new province was to be a tiny one – less than a tenth as large as Lord Selkirk's Assiniboia and about one twenty-fourth its present size. It comprised only the District of Assiniboia, although it was extended to Portage la Prairie. And its name was to be, not Assiniboia (which, it was said, was too confusing) but that of Spence's upstart republic, Manitoba.

The Wolseley Expedition. The Prime Minister gave the impression that the chief purpose of the Wolseley Expedition was to warn off the Americans by a show of strength. Perhaps so, but clearly he had another purpose in mind. Even before the shooting of Scott, he said, "These impulsive halfbreeds must be kept down by a strong hand until they are swamped by the influx of settlers."

The expedition was made up of British regulars and Ontario and Quebec volunteers, although there were apparently fewer than fifty French Canadians among them. The great majority were clearly out for revenge. And even though Colonel Wolseley spoke of a "mission of peace," some of his remarks indicate that he shared much the same view. MacBeth says that if the soldiers had caught Riel "there would have been a lynching."

Wolseley sent an intelligence officer, Captain Butler, ahead of the troops; travelling through the States, Butler reached Red River. But he was at once recognized as a spy and for a week he lived like James Bond (he carried, he says, a "sixteen-shooter"). But he met Riel and later wrote that the Métis chief expressed genuine sympathy for the soldiers − "the poor fellows in their hard journey"; he even wondered whether he should send them guides. Butler noted that Riel regarded himself as the President of a duly elected temporary government, simply waiting to turn over the reins to the vice-regal representative of the Queen.

The troops reached Fort William by ship, but from there they had to battle their way against rocks, swamps, rapids, and mosquitoes, black flies, and deer flies. The vanguard landed at Lower Fort Garry on August 23, in a heavy rain. Wolseley deployed his troops in skirmishing order, and they moved south, ankle-deep in mud, guns at the ready to flush out snipers. On they went, mile after mile, never hearing the crack of a sharp-shooting buffalo hunter's rifle and never being ambushed. On through the village of Winnipeg with its two dozen buildings. And there was the fort − at last − only half a mile on! They regrouped for the attack, and steeled themselves to face its cannon.

Then a strange thing happened. Through the ranks galloped a wild-eyed horseman mounted on a fiery steed. And like Don Quixote jousting at a windmill, he tore straight for the fort. This apparition, they learned later, was James Green Stewart, Chief Factor at Norway House. He had, writes Cowie, been "boiling with indignation" since the surrender of the fort to Riel, and ever since had been drilling his men "so that no such thing should occur at Norway House." And "when he got tired of waiting to be attacked" he "sailed forth (in barges) with his Highland Scots and Swampy Crees to join in the recapture of Fort Garry." At Red River he leaped on a horse and "raced full speed ahead of the troops into the square of Fort Garry in time to utter shouts of wild defiance at Riel and O'Donoghue as they were making their hasty retreat." And, Cowie adds, "Stewart was rewarded (by the HBC) for his war-like ardour by being permitted to retire from the service." Fired!

So this wondrous character had stolen the show from the troops – and after their two months of hardship and revenge-savouring! Except that, as they found when they reached the fort, there was no one there to wreak revenge on. Of course, there were lots of Métis around and it wouldn't be hard to ferret out some of the "guilty" ones. In a few weeks the soldiers of the Queen caused far more casualties than Riel had in ten months. In a Winnipeg saloon, someone pointed out Elezear Goulet: "There's one of the Frogs that shot Scott!" Who had actually made up the firing squad no one will ever know, but naturally Goulet ran, a mob after him. He ran to the river, swam for St. Boniface, and was drowned. In Pembina, Francois Guilmette was killed, and André Nault was bayonetted and left for dead.

If the province's first acknowledged Lieutenant Governor, Adams Archibald (a Nova Scotian), had been there to set up a civil administration, perhaps such crimes would have been prevented. Unfortunately, through a misunderstanding in arrangements, he did not arrive until nine days after the troops. Later he wrote that the Métis were "so beaten and outraged that they felt as if they were living in a state of slavery." There was no punishment for the crimes committed. No witness was going to risk his life by testifying.

So the Riel "rebellion" was over. And in a large sense, Riel and his Métis had won. They had won a great victory for their land rights, language and religion; and they had, by their courage and perseverance, brought a province into being. And, as the American, J.W. Taylor, an observer of all the action, wrote, "Whatever his errors, history will not deny Riel the distinction of being the founder of the Province of Manitoba."

But the Métis had lost too. They could not fight "progress" – the Ontario settlers coming in increasing numbers, the gradual shift from an economy based on hunting to one based on agriculture and commerce. And they could not put a halt to the railway. The life they had loved in the land they loved was ending. The "golden years" were over. Now they could only follow the sun – and the buffalo – westward; and, perhaps, some day, make another stand.

CHAPTER 7

"Go West, Young Man!" (1871-1875)

There were far more French-speaking Catholics in the new province than English-speaking Protestants. So Quebec thought, "Ah, a new western Quebec!" Ontario said, "Just wait and see!" Good land in the East had become scarce, and the young fellows in both provinces knew they could get homesteads in Manitoba for the asking. So they said, "Let's rush out there and pick good ones!" The Quebec lads, on second thought, decided they loved la belle province too much to pull up stakes. But the Ontario lads came in swarms.

The New Legislature. Lieutenant Governor Archibald arranged the first election; and that provided a strange experience – only the immigrants had ever voted before. Most of the electors of course, were non-whites; they made up all but fifteen hundred of the twelve thousand people in the province.

The election was a wild and woolly fight – chiefly because Schultz (who had returned) was running for the Legislature, and he and his "still-loyal" Canadians were still calling for revenge. Schultz ran in Winnipeg against Donald A. Smith, and the voters, supporting Archibald in his efforts to reunite the population, elected Smith.

There was no legislative building yet, so the community-minded A.G.B. Bannatyne allowed the lawmakers to meet in his spacious home, which was east of Main and a little south of Bannatyne Street. In 1922, Mrs. Alex McMicken remembered the ceremonial opening, and what a breathtaking social event it was. The ladies all came dressed in their best; and, she says, so did the Indian women. The squaws walked in solemnly, wearing their best blankets, feathers, and beads.

An Acrobatic Sergeant-at-Arms. Unfortunately, in 1872, Bannatyne's house burned down, as many early wooden structures did
eventually. So the Legislative Chambers were moved to the
second floor of a rickety building over the town jail, a little north
of Bannatyne Street. To reach them it was necessary to climb an
outer stairway and that would make it difficult to conduct the
traditional opening ceremonies. How could the vice-regal representative of the Queen be bowed into the Chambers by the
Sergeant-at-Arms up a rickety stairway? But a provincial legislature was a British Parliament, and all concerned were determined
that these time honoured proceedings should not be dispensed
with. They prepared for the great day – keeping their fingers
crossed.

When it arrived, all those taking part assembled on the sidewalk below. As motley a crowd to be found anywhere in the
world pressed back as the Guards of Honour, stiffly military in
their scarlet uniforms, moved into place. Then the legislators
lined up; some in Prince Alberts, some in capotes, l'Assomption
sashes, and brightly-coloured flannel shirts. And the Sergeant-at-
Arms, bearing the mace, took his position at the bottom of the
stairway.

When all was ready and the crowd was as quiet as it knew
how to be, the Lieutenant Governor, who had been waiting in his
fur-draped sleigh, stepped down – in the full glory of a Windsor
uniform, navy blue and rigid with gold braid; white gloves, dang-
ling dress sword and cocked hat. And up the stairs with great
dignity he walked, but preceded by the Sergeant-at-Arms. Walking backwards! This remarkable fellow was Louis de Plainval,
and he must have practised thoroughly. He walked up backwards, with the mace on his shoulder, bowing every few steps!

If he breathed en route, nobody else did. The spectators, even
those just arrived from the saloon, were fascinated. Then, with
his last safe step, the tension was broken, and there was a collec-
tive letting-out of breath. And applause – and cries of "Atta
boy!" and "Magnifique!"

A Fenian Scare. For years, Red Riverites had heard rumours of
impending raids from Pembina, by wild-eyed Irish Fenians. Just
as the Orangemen were pathetically Protestant and pro-British,
the Fenians were fanatically Catholic and anti-British. In October
of 1871, it almost happened. "General" O'Neill (just out of the

penitentiary) led some thirty of his would-be-avengers across the border. The raid quickly turned into comic opera when American troops appeared and the Fenians disappeared.

But it had an unfortunate side-effect. One of Riel's supporters, the Irish-American W.B. O'Donoghue had instigated the raid, and this gave Schultz an opportunity to spew more venom – "More rebellion by the French!"

Both the English and the French, who were still led by Riel had taken down their buffalo guns, ready to fight off any real invasion. But the French, it seems, were a little late in offering their services, and the haters of all Catholics, Fenian or French, noted this with relish. Archibald felt (as he wrote later) that if the French had joined the Fenians, there would have been civil war, that the timing did not matter, and that therefore the French should be thanked. So he crossed to St. Boniface and, at an inspection of Métis troops, shook hands with their leader – who, in view of the circumstances, carefully remained anonymous. He was, of course, Louis Riel, for whose capture rewards had been posted in the East. Archibald had played right into the hands of the haters, and now they yelled, not only for Riel's head but for Archibald's too.

Bishop Taché maintained that the Dominion government had promised amnesty for all the resisters. But it now seemed clear that there could be no peace in Manitoba if a full amnesty were granted, and none if it were denied. Prime Minister Macdonald came up with at least a temporary solution. Knowing that the problem would not solve itself, he arranged, through Taché, for Riel to go away – for $4,000, to be shared with his lieutenant, Lepine. The two left the country. "The province," says one writer, "lapsed into a state of quietude." It was also without Lieutenant Governor Adams Archibald. Violent attacks had been made on him by newspapers in Ontario: the Toronto *Globe* accused him of being "an Englishman acting like a Frenchman, a Protestant behaving like a Catholic." And in Manitoba enough citizens had been led on by Schultz and his lads to make the position of this man of integrity impossible. So he left as well.

Reaching the West. The East had been hearing tales for years about the "fabulous" West. Some of them, though, sounded as if they had been made up by fathers to keep their sons from being lured away. You couldn't grow a crop because the season was

98

too short; wheat would be blackened by frost in August – if it hadn't been eaten by grasshoppers – or if you hadn't been eaten by wolves. If you survived the summer, the winter would get you. You would have to spend the summer hauling wood – if you could find any on the bald prairie. And you would need a roaring fire in a huge stove to keep from being frozen stiff. One writer reckoned it would take five cords of wood to court a girl.

Letters from "out West" told a different story. Wheat had been harvested – good, hard wheat – sixty bushels to the acre! As for vegetables: potatoes weighing five pounds, turnips thirty pounds, one onion alone weighing over eighteen pounds, and cabbage four feet around! Exaggerated or not, such glowing reports made many a young fellow heed Horace Greeley's advice: "Go West, young man!"

But getting out there was not easy. You could reach Moorhead by rail, but from there you had to go by Shank's mare, or scrounge a ride with a cart brigade. If it was spring, you could build a raft and let the spring floods carry you north. If you had a little money, you could take a steamer: by 1875, there were eleven chugging sternwheelers doing a roaring freight and passenger business.

Some of these steamboats were almost as makeshift as the *Anson Northup* had been. Mark Twain is said to have sailed on one, and in a piece he wrote later he says that the long smokestack drew such a fierce draft that when the Negro fireman (this makes it sound like a Mississippi story) opened the door of the firebox to throw in a log, he'd be sucked in, and up – and out! This happened so regularly that he took to wearing his bathing suit while firing!

They were all flat-bottomed, these sternwheelers, and as the country along the snaky river was also flat, some strange things happened. One spring the water was so high that one of the smaller craft sailed off over the river bank – turned off the regular route – and proceeded to take a short cut across the prairie. In the flood of 1882, the *Cheyenne* sailed right up the main street of the bustling new town of Emerson and unloaded its cargo of lumber on the steps of the Presbyterian Church.

If you were going to settle far from the main streams, you had to cross the prairie by oxcart, prairie schooner, buckboard or horseback. Pat Burns, founder of the beef-packing firm, walked a hundred miles to his homestead. Some of these would-be sod-

busters had narrow escapes from prairie fires or stampeding buffalo, and many told of hair-raising escapes from Indians. Most of the Indian tales brought smiles from those who had lived among the "savages" – like the famous missionaries, John McDougall and Father Lacombe. Indians, they said, were dangerous only when on the warpath. But they loved a joke, and one of their favourites was scaring the living daylights out of greenhorn palefaces.

There were sternwheelers on the Assiniboia too. But this river was so shallow that sometimes in dry periods they couldn't get past the St. James rapids. The water level, in fact, seems to have been the ship captains' chief concern. According to one story, a captain, seeing a settler on shore dipping out water with a pail, shouted, "Hey you, put that water back!" And the Assiniboine was as winding as the Red. A crow flying from Winnipeg to Fort Pelly (north of the present Kamsack) would fly 400 miles; the boats had to sail 1,000 miles. Some of the curves in the river doubled back so far that, to relieve the tedium of a long trip, passengers would sometimes disembark, walk straight across the "peninsula" – and wait for their boat to pick them up. The trip from Winnipeg to Portage took four or five days; you could walk the distance in two.

As in all immigration movements, women played a vital role. A newspaper reporter visiting Manitoba quipped that the West was a place where "men are men and women are back East." He must have been thinking of unmarried men and women; most wives came with their husbands. Some of these would be ex-city girls, and the reporter wrote that in Winnipeg he had talked to many a "tenderfoot" lady "not cut out for the life . . . they were shaped like hourglasses, with too many petticoats and too much hair . . . and they hadn't the faintest idea of how to hitch up a span of oxen." All the more credit to them if they "stuck" it, which most of them did. They crossed the prairies in Red River carts or swaying covered wagons, they faced flood and drought and "forty below," they lived in sod houses, and they often made homes for their men and their children under primitive, seemingly impossible conditions.

Many immigrants came from the States. Fifty years later, Mrs. C.P. Brown recalled travelling for forty days by prairie schooner from Iowa, and her father pitching their tent on the site of Winnipeg's present City Hall. Then they moved on to Palestine (now Gladstone), thus becoming the "farthest west" settlers on the prairies. Mrs. John McQuade remembered her father buying a parcel of land in Winnipeg in the 1870's for ten dollars and selling it in the 1900's for ten thousand dollars. Mrs. McQuade had nine children but "no doctor ever entered our house and they all grew up."

The Mennonites: First on the Open Prairie. There were raised eyebrows at the sight of the first Mennonites: "Foreigners!" Women wearing aprons and with handkerchiefs around their heads! And the men with their long beards and sheepskin coats! But when the Anglo-Saxons found that the peasants were paying for their supplies in gold, the eyebrows came down. And Mennonite stock went up still higher when they courageously settled on the unproven "bald prairie" and produced excellent crops. In 1876, J.C. McLagan wrote:

> Seldom have I beheld any spectacle more pregnant with prophecy, more fraught with promise of a successful future, than the Mennonite settlement. When I visited these people, they had been only two years in the province, and yet, in a long ride I took across many miles of prairies, which but yesterday were absolutely bare – the home of the wolf, the badger, and the eagle – I passed village after village, homestead after homestead, furnished with all the conveniences of European comfort and a scientific agriculture, while on either side of the road cornfields already ripe for harvest, and pastures populous with herds of cattle, stretched away to the horizon.

The New Vikings. In 1875, the first party of Icelandic immigrants arrived. These were mostly young descendants of the Vikings, who had discovered America five hundred years before Columbus. They chose Willow Point on the western shore of Lake Winnipeg as their new home, called it Gimli ("Paradise"), after floating their few belongings down the Red and along the lake. The men built log huts, some then walking back to Selkirk or Winnipeg to find work to tide them over.

At that time the Gimli area was outside Manitoba's original

northern limits, which ended at today's Winnipeg Beach's Boundary Creek. There they drew up a constitution, and until the borders were extended in 1881, they were allowed to conduct their own affairs as the Republic of New Iceland.

If the Icelanders were – at least when they arrived – short of cash, they were long on culture, and they have been an asset to the province far greater than their small numbers might suggest. Although they have never, through the years, made up much more than two per cent of the province's population, the number of individuals who have become prominent in science (the explorer, Stefansson, for example), medicine, law, government and education is almost unbelievable.

Winnipeg: a Hive of Industry. In 1871, the few businesses in the village of Winnipeg were stores (one was a taxless, rentless, flatboat store on the Red), a saw mill, hotels, and saloons. But soon there was a bakery, factories making furniture, carriages, bricks, and several more sawmills. And a branch of the Merchants Bank, the manager of which, according to a story, had travelled west with $200,000 sewn into the lining of his vest. By 1875, the HBC had built a "mammoth mill" for grinding grain, and the property which Henry McKenney had bought for $550 sold for $15,000. In 1877, E.L. Drewry opened his brewery near the present Redwood Bridge. By then there were far more saloons – full of unbelievable characters from all over the world doing a roaring business.

The most thriving industry, throughout the 1870's and 1880's, was housebuilding. Contractors could never hire enough skilled workers, partly because the men got only ten to twenty cents an hour. Houses could be, and often were, built in twenty-four hours, but the prospective occupants usually had to wait and live in tents. In fact, the first impression new arrivals got was that this was a "city of tents."

The first stage line from the south began operating in 1871, and soon there was a tri-weekly mail and passenger service. The same year a great event: the long-hoped-for telegraph line to Pembina! Winnipeg was no longer an isolated "island."

How strange all this must have seemed to the surviving Selkirk settlers who could remember the trip from York Factory to the Forks and the Battle of Seven Oaks! Actually, some of the old ways hadn't vanished. In 1873, Hon. W.J. Christie arrived in

103

Winnipeg from Fort Simpson, two thousand miles north, by dog team. And two hundred Indians held their annual dog-meat feast not far from the scene of Seven Oaks. No wonder a writer visiting Winnipeg entitled his article for an American magazine, "My Journey to the End of the World."

Even though the village of Winnipeg was growing fast, everyday life for most families was still unhurried. The men's chief diversion was smoking red willow bark, drinking, and bandying words with cronies (especially about politics) in the Red Saloon or the Davis House. In summer, a man might take his dog and go hunting. There was lots of game, even moose, as close as Lower Fort Garry. Geese were the most valuable of all game: they provided meat − salted down or frozen for the winter, feathers and down for pillows and ticks, quills for pens, and goose grease for many ailments.

Fishing was good sport and profitable too, and there were a dozen species of fish to go after. Goldeyes were plentiful, but they had not become the gourmet's item they are today because the Indian trick of smoking them (which, incidentally, is what turns them red) hadn't been learned. Sturgeon, providing oil for lamps as well as food, weighed up to eighty pounds, and in some cases much more! A woman once drowned trying to land one. Strange as it may seem, this particular sturgeon may still be eluding fishermen; in the 1960's, a sturgeon caught in Manitoba waters was estimated to be 150 years old − maybe it was one of those that got away from, say, Lord Selkirk in the summer of 1817.

In the long winters, people had to think up things to do. There was much skating on the river. In the snowless winter of 1877, Charles N. Bell, Wolseley's, "bugle boy," and champion fancy skater "from Ontario," skated from Winnipeg to Selkirk.

Most winter nights were spent at home, doing the household chores and taking care of the family pet, perhaps a fox tied to a long chain, or a baby deer or buffalo or a cinnamon bear; and reading the weekly *Manitoban,* or the *Free Press* which started in 1872. All the time, of course, they were dreaming of that great day, the day the ice on the river would go out, as that would signal the imminent arrival of the first steamboat of the season to visit their isolated part of the world.

Each succeeding winter they had reason to feel less lonely because more and more farmers' sons were coming West. That

104

meant more people with skills and ideas. It also meant that whenever a family man with marriageable daughters arrived he had no trouble pairing them off within a few weeks, even days. One brought five daughters, all adept at sewing, and these "animated sewing machines," as a reporter called them, were all snapped up. So there were lots of weddings at which to celebrate. At one wedding the bridegroom changed his mind and lit out for the prairie. But a handsome spectator stepped up; the bride said, like Barkis, that she was "willin'," and the lad got himself a wife – without even trying.

Characters in a "Wicked" City. "Winnipeg is getting too big for its britches!" said a Kildonan man in 1873. If he meant that the businessmen of the village felt that it was becoming big enough and important enough to be allowed to run its local affairs, he was right. "Winnipeg is going to be a city," they told every other Winnipegger who would listen, "so let's demand that the Legislature incorporate it – now!" They did; they proceeded to hold mass meetings and torchlight parades to impress the lawmakers. And at last a bill of incorporation was brought up – to be turned down. So now the citizens held indignation meetings, accused the few wealthy property owners of opposing them, fearing heavy taxes, and burned the effigies of Donald A. Smith, the wealthiest of them all, and other "bigwigs." A gang, which set out to tar and feather the Attorney General, apparently couldn't find any feathers – or the Attorney General. Instead, they waylaid and tarred the unoffending Speaker of the House.

The Members of the Legislature, no doubt shaking in their boots, held special sessions to reconsider. And on the critical day the embattled citizens jammed into the Chambers, only to find that most of the lawmakers had left in a hurry, some to buy revolvers. When they returned, they passed the Bill in no time flat. And so, in November, 1873, Winnipeg, with a population of 1,869, became a city.

Of course, the "city" was still a frontier town, with no local laws, no taxes, and too many saloons. A reporter from the East wrote that Winnipeg and Barrie, Ontario, were "the wickedest places in Canada." At a YMCA convention prayers were offered for both cities. Actually there was little serious crime in Winnipeg, mostly "horseplay." Its one great "crime," all agreed, was "too much mud." The community was famous for its mud. In

wet weather the few patches of wooden sidewalk, to quote a visitor, "floated like barges." One storekeeper resorted to walking to his store in his bare feet, carrying his polished shoes. And newcomers were told that if they ever saw a hat floating in the mud, they were to throw it a line – there would be a man under it.

But a city has to have a Mayor, so, the ruction-raising citizens elected one of the least inhibited of their cronies, Frank Cornish, Q.C. (He had offered many a housewife a goose for Christmas if she would persuade her husband to vote for him.) As Mayor he proved appropriately imaginative. A story has it that, sitting one morning as Police Magistrate, he laid a charge against himself for drunken driving (horse and carriage). Then he left the chair, stood with bowed head before that seat of justice, said "Guilty, Your Honour!", resumed his place, fined himself five dollars – then immediately remitted the fine as this was his first offence.

Many of the early elections, if a bit irregular, were hilarious – at least to read about. In the Cornish election, there were 388 voters on the lists – but 562 votes were cast, most of them for Cornish. Voting was open and Cornish's bully-boys had done a thorough job. In another election, he didn't like the way things were going, so he and his pals "visited" the house of the chief polling officer, there was a scuffle and they came away with the polling book. In still another election, two close friends found themselves pitted against each other for Mayor. They proceeded to make history: they plugged for each other. Each became eloquent on the character and ability of his opponent. And, of course, the more eloquent candidate won – he got his opponent elected.

Yet the new City Council got things done. A start was made in constructing a sewage system. In 1874 a police force was established; its first notable arrest: Chief of Police Ingram (who was caught in a brothel). In 1875, a City Hall was built (in the cornerstone, among the documents: a jar of grasshoppers pickled in alcohol). A modern fire engine was bought, and when it burned to twisted metal, along with the fire house, the City Fathers bought another. To have water to fight fires, they built, at strategic spots, twenty-one huge underground tanks, one of which was discovered under Lombard Street in 1950.

A fire in those days was heralded like a stage play. Chief McRobie, on his fast horse, galloped ahead, blasting the news on his bugle. After a fire he would ride right into the bar of the

Queen's Hotel and order whiskey – with beer for his horse.

But there were real stage plays too, put on in the loft over Lyon's feed store. Both actors and audience risked their lives; the building was so weak that Lyons had a notice up: "The audience is requested not to applaud for fear the building will collapse." Plays and many other kinds of entertainment were also put on in the City Hall. In fact, a walking race was staged there; it lasted for forty-eight hours, the winner covering 151 miles.

The first City Hall was built over Brown's creek, which crossed Main Street near William Avenue. The Councillors had tried to save money by using the creek bed for the cellars of the building. But it let them down – rather let the building down. In 1886 they replaced it with the rugged "gingerbread" structure which could have lasted indefinitely, but was demolished in 1964 to make way for a third civic administration centre.

A "Titled" Impostor: Lord Gordon Gordon. In the middle 70's, Winnipeggers enjoyed a real life drama. A handsome young Scot, calling himself Lord Gordon Gordon, arrived in town and, with his aristocratic manner and dress, aroused the interest and curiosity of the whole population. A real Lord in Winnipeg! Why? Apparently annoyed by such attention he moved out of town; he took lodgings at the house of Mrs. Abigail Corbett at Headingly, hired her nephew, Thomas Pentland, as his "man," and settled down to the life of a country squire.

But the mystery increased, fed by Pentland. That many-coloured "wes'coat" the Lord always wore? He had $50,000 sewn into the lining! And that bulge in his coat? A loaded pistol that he always placed on his bed table at night!

Months went by, then finally the mystery was solved. He was on the run. And he wasn't a Lord; he was plain Private Tom Smith of the British army. He had simply thought up a better way to make a fast buck. In Minneapolis he had rooked the Northern Pacific Railway out of $100,000; in New York he had taken Jay Gould, one of the racketeering railway-tycoons of the time, for half a million.

He must have felt safe at this Canadian outpost, because he didn't change his name or appearance. But one day a businessman from Minneapolis recognized him and got in touch with Gould. Gould arranged to have two policemen go to Winnipeg – armed with an *American* warrant – to bring the culprit back.

The two constables, Hoy and Keegan, arrived and held a pre-arrest conference with three Minnesota businessmen – Fletcher, Merriam and Bentley – who were in on the deal. But they all began to feel some doubt about the validity of their American warrant. So they changed their plan. Hoy and Keegan wouldn't arrest their man; they would simply capture him and take him back to the States by force. That night they drove out to Headingly in a buckboard and as luck would have it, they found Gordon alone, sitting on the veranda. They held a pistol to his head, bound and gagged him, tossed him into the buckboard and set out for the border.

But the plot was discovered and the Provincial Attorney General, Hon. H.J. Clarke, telegraphed the Canadian customs officer, Frank Bradley, at the border. Bradley and his assistant came upon the two Americans camped by the trail, got the drop on them and sent them back to Winnipeg under guard. The next thing the Minneapolis law men knew, they were in jail, along with Fletcher, Merriam and Bentley, all of them charged with kidnapping.

Fletcher and Mayor Brackett of Minneapolis had agreed on a code. If the plot failed, Fletcher was to wire: "Too high; can't purchase; have written." Fletcher sent his telegram, then followed it with a much more down-to-earth wire: "I'm in a hell of a fix. Come at once." The next day Brackett was speeding north with two lawyers. By this time both Ottawa and Washington had been informed of the situation. The atmosphere was becoming charged.

When the prisoners were brought to trial, the decision of the court was that they were to be held over for the Fall Assizes. Held for weeks in jail! The news was trumpeted on the front page of the newspapers in the States and brought hysterical protests. The St. Paul *Pioneer* denounced the "crime" being committed by this "mock" Canadian court; it urged that a rescue plan be devised that would be "swift, silent and terrible"; that Gordon should be recaptured; that Manitoba should be "wrapped in flames."

There was action as well as outcry. Minnesota's Governor Austin, along with Mayor Brackett, rushed to Washington and appealed to the Secretary of State, who gave them slight comfort; and to the British ambassador, who gave them none. But by the middle of August, reports from Ottawa showed that pressure from Washington was beginning to be felt. The Governor General, Lord Dufferin, and Prime Minister Macdonald both declared that bail would simply have to be granted to clear the air.

By September the pressure was so great that an explosion seemed imminent. But there was no explosion; there was a terrific anti-climax. Someone said, "Why not just have the prisoners plead guilty and recieve a light sentence?" The judge – maybe they suddenly saw the humour of the situation – bowed in agreement.

So with everything already cut and dried, a puppet-trial was staged, with Governor Austin, an invited guest, sitting smiling on the bench beside the judge. The formalities were over in a minute. The prisoners were declared guilty as charged and sentenced to twenty-four hours in jail. And everybody went home happy.

Then Gould got smart. He secured a *Canadian* warrant, and two private detectives from Toronto arrived in Winnipeg. They drove out to the Headingly house, knocked on the door and asked for Lord Gordon Gordon. When he appeared they requested him to return with them to Toronto to answer several charges. With his usual masterly composure Gordon bowed, went to his bedroom, picked up his pistol – and shot himself through the head.

CHAPTER 8

John A., Donald A. and the CPR (1875-1882)

Sir John A. Macdonald succeeded in getting a CPR *company started, but both his government and the company were wrecked by the Pacific Scandal of 1873. The head of the new Liberal government, Alexander Mackenzie, was appalled at the cost of a trans-Canada railway and decided to build it piece-meal. Manitoba was appalled too – at the thought of waiting. At this point Donald A., who had been chiefly responsible for the defeat of John's government, entered the scene. He persuaded Mackenzie to grant him a charter for a line from Winnipeg to Pembina to connect with an American line. Manitobans were – temporarily – happy.*

At the time, there was no American railway running up to Pembina. But Donald A. had got wind of a line, the St. Paul & Pacific, which had gone bankrupt. And hoping to secure financial backing to buy it, he asked his cousin, George Stephen, President of the Bank of Montreal, if he would come with him to St. Paul and investigate. The story is that Stephen flipped a coin and it came up heads; the end result was that he and his enterprising cousin – two Scots turned Canadian – teamed up with James J. Hill and Norman Kittson – two Canadians turned American – to take over the American line. So the toss of a coin, if the story is true, resulted in Manitoba getting rail connection through the States with the East. And in eventually adding a hundred million or so to Donald's fortune.

The news that there was going to be a railway up from the States was followed by an announcement that Lord Dufferin, Governor General of Canada, and Lady Dufferin were coming on a tour. Their visit proved a memorable one. That the Dufferins

111

were genuine, interested people is evident in the writings of Lady Dufferin in her *Journal*. They journeyed (in a day when travel was no pleasure) to a Mennonite settlement (near the present Winkler) where they were greeted by seven hundred Mennonites standing on the prairie holding specimens of their farm and garden produce. They visited the Icelanders at Gimli and the Indians at St. Peter's. Their visit to the penitentiary at Stony Mountain was quite an event. For the last half mile they rode, through a series of triumphal arches, in a Red River cart drawn by eighty oxen. The remark made by Lady Dufferin on the institution was that its operation must have been expensive: there were fourteen officials – and fourteen prisoners!

One Manitoban that Lady Dufferin seems to have found fascinating above all others was James McKay, part Indian, and a giant of a man. He made her hair stand on end, she says, with his story of how he killed a bear with a lasso. Having no gun with him at the time, he threw his lasso over his head, turned his horse away quickly, pulled the bear over on its back and strangled it. She also notes that though he weighed three hundred and twenty pounds, he was light on his feet, and at the Lieutenant Governor's ball (to which he came dressed as Falstaff) taught her the Red River Jig.

Meanwhile, work was going ahead on the branch line to Pembina. It was to run on the east side of the Red, and as there was no bridge to Winnipeg, the terminal was to be at St. Boniface. Just before the Dufferins left the province, they crossed to St. Boniface on the new steam ferry and drove the first two spikes. Then they left for Ottawa on the sternwheeler *Minnesota* – "amidst much firing and shouting and waving adieux."

Three days later, at Fisher's Landing, Lady Dufferin wrote: "We went ashore and saw the engine of the Canada Pacific Railway. It is going to Winnipeg . . . and is to be called the 'Lady Dufferin.' " A week later Winnipeggers were startled, and agog with excitement, when the *Selkirk* came 'round the bend towing a barge with a locomotive (later christened "Lady Dufferin") and several flat cars on board! They were all decorated with Union Jacks, Stars and Stripes, and streamers of bunting. The now-famous locomotive had steam up, and says a record of the time, "What with its shrill whistling and that of the steamer, the ringing of bells and the whistles of the sawmills joining in the chorus, there was a perfect babel of noise." And "a young lady, Miss

Racine, kept ringing the bell of the steamer, and was cheered lustily by the crowd."

The Pembina line was ready to operate in late 1878, except for one final ceremony. One day a party of dignitaries and their wives seated themselves on one of the flat cars which had been decorated all over again; they were journeying to what someone called a "rendezvous with history": the driving of the last spike. But *en route* a crisis of a kind arose: which one of them was to actually drive the spike? Nobody had been officially appointed. Someone suggested that it be one of the ladies. Fine, but which lady?

Fortunately, Winnipeg's supreme diplomat, James W. Taylor, the American consul, was aboard, and he said simply, "Why, *each* lady!" Crisis solved. Only to be followed, at the historic spot, by still another: no lady was going to risk losing her look of "fragility" just to drive an old spike, so each of them in turn lifted the mallet and just dropped it daintily on the spike. Some were so concerned with how they looked they even missed the spike. But again the diplomat came to the rescue. Turning to the husky daughter of the section foreman, he smiled and said, "Please!" and handed her the mallet. She glanced at the spike, then with one mighty blow drove it home. Thus was Western Canada's railway age ushered in.

Driving last spikes was usually restricted to dignitaries (thus the section boss's daughter could be said to have "struck a blow" for democracy. But anyone with a few dollars could aspire to ride a first train. The greatest prize would be not just a ticket, but the *first* ticket sold. It went to Sam Shorey, a clothing merchant; the priceless document, all in handwriting, is still in the possession of the family.

Sam's trip south (December, 1878) was unique in another sense. As there was no turntable at St. Boniface, the engine had to be driven, as someone quipped, "southwards backwards." All Winnipeggers on the train had had to get to St. Boniface on their own. St. Boniface was temporarily the West's rail centre: Winnipeg was just one of its suburbs. There was seasonal rail connection of a sort between the two: a line of track, supported by double-length ties, was laid on the river ice and trains crossed all winter.

That, incidentally, wouldn't have been possible the previous year. It was Manitoba's mildest, before or since; on December

23, 1877, the thermometer shot up to 47.2 above zero. It was so mild that it confused the game birds. Ducks and geese were still around in late December and hunters went out for fresh meat. Some sleigh-drivers must have been confused, too: they drove their teams onto the river and went through the ice. On Christmas day the farmers at Scratching River held a plowing match; and on New Year's day, Winnipeg staged a sports day, with the athletes in short sleeves and short pants.

The CPR! *Coming for Sure!* In 1878, Macdonald's Conservatives defeated MacKenzie's Liberals and were returned to power. In the West, even Liberals cried, "Ah, now we'll get an all-Canadian railway!" John A.'s opponents had long labelled him "Old Tomorrow," and "the Prince of Procrastinators," but he did not put off the CPR. A syndicate was formed, headed by Smith, Stephen and Hill, and in an amazingly short time, construction was under way.

Strange as it may seem, the birth of the trans-Canada railway – that is, the decision eventually to raise the money – had taken place eight years earlier. Donald A., returning east from Red River, travelled by dog-sled through Minnesota. One afternoon in a blizzard, another dog-sled party, travelling north, appeared. The two parties decided to camp together for safety – and Donald A. met James J. Hill for the first time.

The two men shared a tent and talked far into the night. What they decided they apparently kept to themselves – for forty years. Only at a luncheon in Winnipeg in 1909, at which they were both guests of honour, did they tell the story. Said Donald A., now Lord Strathcona: "On that bitter night in 1870, in a tent on the frozen prairie, the Canadian Pacific Railway was born."

Winnipeggers had taken it for granted that the main line would cross the Red at Winnipeg. They were jolted when in 1874 the engineers recommended a place that didn't even have a name: they called it "The Crossing." When the CPR began building its Western offices there, people rushed to buy land around it – to be "in on the ground floor." Soon there were stores, hotels, a school, and its new citizens, confident that the place was destined to become a city, chose a new name for it – a name with great prestige – Selkirk. Within a year or so they even started a newspaper, with the expansive title, *The Inter-Ocean.*

Winnipeg's City Councillors "pulled every string" to have the

Selkirk recommendation ignored. They suspected, and they were probably right, that the fact that the city did not already have a railway bridge over the river had worked against it. Or, at least, having one would have worked for it. So they should have at once persuaded their taxpayers to vote money to build on. Instead they tried to persuade the Mackenzie government to supply the funds – and failed. When Mackenzie himself failed to stay in power, Winnipeg opened negotiations with John A.'s new government and the new Canadian Pacific Railway Company.

John A. and Donald A. and their cohorts had Winnipeg "over a barrel" because it wanted the railway so badly. So they said, "Build your own bridge." They did not say, "If you build your own bridge, the railway will run over it"; there were all kinds of "wheels within wheels" complexities in the situation. But whatever the reasons, the end result was the same: Winnipeg won the prize by building the bridge. "The Crossing" would be, not at Selkirk, but Winnipeg.

As was to be expected, the prize had price strings attached. It had to grant the company exemption from municipal taxation in perpetuity ("perpetuity" ended, at least in theory, in 1965), and it had to grant "right of way" and land for station and yards. The revenue the city lost, up to 1965, was, in turn, small change compared with the hundreds of millions it gained over the years; insignificant, in view of the fact that becoming "The Crossing" eventually made it the metropolis of the West. Winnipeg had triumphed – "in perpetuity."

Why had Winnipeg won? One historian contends that the decision was a triumph of "public opinion" over the judgment of engineers. Another thinks that possibly Donald A., who was now the HBC's top man in Canada, had succeeded in "pulling the right strings" – the choice of Winnipeg would greatly enhance the value of the HBC's extensive acreage in almost the centre of Winnipeg. It wouldn't be through love for the city: his 1879 bid to represent the constituency at Ottawa had been upset by the courts because of corrupt practices, for which he blamed Winnipeg and never forgave it.

The real reason for changing may have been a major policy decision to run the main CPR line closer to the border to prevent too many American branch lines being built into Canadian territory.

Winnipeggers were so ecstatic at the news that, as one writer said, they might have built the bridge themselves if skilled workers hadn't been available. When the project was finished, they named it Louise Bridge, in honour of a daughter of Queen Victoria. On July 26, 1881, a CPR train from the East first used it to cross the Red River into Winnipeg.

This was a day for the history books! A century and a half earlier, the arrival of La Vérendrye had established the canoe route from Montreal; then in 1821, with the end of the NWC, the connection had been broken. Now it was reforged in steel. And just as the forks of the Red and Assiniboine had been the distributing and supply depot for the fur trade, so it would be for agriculture and industry.

The Boom. Ever since the early 1870's, land had been in good demand: land for *use*. When the CPR was assured and the trickle of settlers rose to a flood, the speculative buying and selling of land became hectic. "Manitoba Land Fever" had broken out, and the result was the most spectacular event in Winnipeg's or Manitoba's history – "The Boom" – during the years 1881 and 1882.

"Speculators poured in from all over the continent," wrote Edith Paterson in the *Free Press* recently, quoting early newspaper accounts, "and they held property auctions day and night anywhere and everywhere, even from the back of a buckboard. Canvas-topped sleighs, painted with pictures of golden cities, patrolled the streets, with bells ringing and barkers touting the auctions. . . . Property in Emerson went on the auction-block as far away as Halifax. . . . Specimens of Manitoba soil were on display in the capitals of Europe." Lots were brazenly advertised in non-existent towns – even swamps; Hingston Smith's offered for sale "special surveyors' snowshoes, five feet long." One dealer brought in fifteen hundred tents; another advertised "good sleeping accommodation" in "Taylor's Tent" – on March 15. To help celebrate, "G.F. and J. Galt announced the arrival of a carload of champagne in a specially heated car."

Principal Grant, of Queen's University, wrote: "Winnipeg is London or New York on a small scale. Friends meet who parted last on the other side of the globe, and with a hasty 'What! You here, too?' each passes on his way, probably to a real estate office or auction room. The writer saw Winnipeg first in 1872. It consisted of a few rickety-looking shanties that looked as if they had been dropped promiscuously on the verge of a boundless prairie. The poorest inhabitant seemed willing to *give* anyone a lot or an acre. And now, land on Main Street and the streets adjoining is held at higher figures than in the centre of Toronto; and Winnipeggers, in referring to the future, never make comparisons with any city smaller than Chicago."

Land was sold like any commodity. Says R.B. Hill: "A craze seemed to have come over the mass of the people. Legitimate business in many cases was thrown aside and buying and selling lots became the one aim and object of life. Carpenters, painters, tailors and tradesmen of all kinds threw aside their tools to open real estate offices. . . . Crowds smashed windows to get into them." Wrote newsman George Ham, "If there ever was a fool's paradise it sure was Winnipeg."

Another visitor wrote: "Winnipeg has 45 hotels, 300 boarding houses and I defy any man twice out of five times to strike a night's lodging. The immigrants are pouring in. I got a good room, but if I want to go up to it at ten o'clock in the evening, I have to step over the sleeping forms in the halls and on the stairs. In the woodbox, under the billiard tables – everywhere, you will find them – and yet there have only arrived three or four immigrant trains. There are seven more stuck in a snowbank near Chicago. I hope, for my own convenience, they will remain there two or three weeks."

The early part of the winter of 1881-82 saw the boom at its height. There were three hundred real estate dealers in Winnipeg, forty in Portage la Prairie. One of the most successful, if unscrupulous, in the selling of real estate, was an Irish-Canadian named Jim Coolican. He sold so many lots on muddy Main Street that he got the name "The Marquis de Mud." His auction mart in a ramshackle building near the corner of Portage and Main was like a Barnum and Bailey circus; in two weeks he sold a million dollars' worth of lots. Coolican was of Falstaffian proportions, with red cheeks and a flowing black moustache, and eyes that twinkled like the huge diamonds he sported on both hands. In winter he wore a sealskin coat for which he was said to have paid $5,000. Among the stories about him was one that whenever he made an especially big "killing" he rejoiced in a champagne bath.

The boom became more and more fantastic until April, 1882. One Friday, lots were eagerly being bought – as far west as

118

Edmonton – and at high prices. On Saturday, the buyers were frantically trying to get rid of them, at any price. The bubble had collapsed! Those who had expected to make fortunes, which meant practically everybody, found themselves broke. As one writer put it, "Men who had lived in a dream of Oriental magnificence, now dwelt in the sad valley of humiliation."

Stephen Leacock's Remarkable Uncle. E.P. Leacock was not one of this unfortunate multitude. His novel way of surviving has been told in a book which Stephen Leacock wrote called *My Remarkable Uncle*. The uncle (E.P.) actually lived.

"E.P.," Leacock writes, was "a man of the world, bronzed and self-confident." And "his character was so exaggerated already that you couldn't exaggerate it." He had been in some of the Mediterranean countries and "his talk was of Algiers and the West African slave market." To his young nephew in Canada, it sounded like something from *The Arabian Nights*.

In practically no time at all after hitting Winnipeg, E.P. "knew everybody and was in everything. He became president of a bank, a brewery, and a railway, all of them existing only on paper." He called the railway "The Winnipeg, Hudson Bay and Arctic Ocean Railway," and he had passes printed and sent to the heads of real railways. Which meant, of course, that E.P. received passes good all over the continent – and he used them! He "went to Toronto with the Premier of the province and other politicos, all in heavy buffalo coats and bearded like Assyrians, and paraded on King Street like a returned explorer with savages." And he brought back a charming wife. Then he built a large house on the bank of the Red, filled it with pictures that he said were of his ancestors – one of them a Portuguese duke – and carried on a roaring hospitality that never stopped.

When the boom collapsed he went right on: he just used credit instead of cash. His roaring hospitality still roared, and the shop-owners paid for it. If a collector called at the great house about a bill, E.P.'s "men" would inform him loftily, imperially, that the great man was "in conference," that his future movements were uncertain at the moment. He might be called away any day to Johannesburg – it would depend a good deal on what happened in West Africa! Or E.P. himself might appear and say, "My dear fellow, I'm told your name is Framley! Then surely you must be a relation of my dear old friend General Sir Charles Framley of the Horse Artillery!" The poor flattered collector could only grin foolishly. And E.P. would end the interview with, "I must tell Sir Charles I've seen you . . . he'll be so pleased!"

Inevitably E.P.'s own private crash came. His credit crumbled, friends turned their faces away, and at last the crowning indignity: he was thrown out of a saloon.

That was too much. His great spirit broke, he ended his days humbly back in England. No cable had called him imperially to West Africa. But he was not forgotten by his admiring nephew, and Stephen Leacock ends his piece by saying that he doesn't think of him as just a humbug. What is more, says Stephen, he is sure E.P. will go straight to heaven. And at the Golden Gates he will look at St. Peter and say, "Peter? Then surely you must be a relation of Lord Peter of Titchfield!" And St. Peter would let him in.

The West was full of such "remarkable uncles."

CHAPTER 9

The "Wars" of the Eighties and Nineties (1882-1900)

Many people today still remember their grandparents reminiscing about the "old days," when people were irrepressibly lighthearted in facing the hardships of frontier life. So they were, of course; but there was conflict aplenty, especially in a new country where new relationships had to be worked out. So inevitably, there were many clashes between competing interests: "Wars" of one kind or another were being waged all the time.

The Wiping Out of the Buffalo. One of these "wars" was not against people, but against the buffalo, which was eventually exterminated. Not by the Indians; they hardly made a dent in their vast numbers. Nor even by the Métis. The disappearance of the buffalo was probably due, to a large extent, to the American railways, which kept gangs of sharpshooters systematically slaughtering them; Buffalo Bill is said to have once shot sixty a minute for almost an hour. One scientist feels that the terrible blizzards and deep snow of 1880-81 might have had much to do with finishing them off. In 1880, there were still large numbers: by 1882, there were only a scattered few.

A tragedy to the Indian! For the hunter of the plains the great beast had provided not just pemmican but every necessity of life. Its skin made his tepee and his coat, his bridle and his lariat; it even served as a boat for crossing streams – when stretched on a hoop made of willows. He used its horns for a powder-flask and its sinews for bow-strings. The buffalo robe had been his carpet and his bed in life, and his shroud in death. Now the Indian, riding listlessly over the plains, would see only bleaching bones. A few years later he would see the white man's "iron horse"

pulling carloads of bones to Chicago to be used in the bleaching of sugar and making of fertilizer. The old order had indeed changed.

If there are thousands of buffalo in parks all over the continent today – so many that they have to be thinned out occasionally – it is because a few men were farsighted enough to save a small number of calves. James Mackay was one of them; he brought eight calves to his farm at Deer Lodge and allowed them to pasture with his cattle. Years later, stockmen in Canada and the United States bred buffalo to domestic cattle, hoping to produce a hardier breed of beef-cow. They got a hybrid they called a "cattalo"; then found that the males were always sterile. Buffalo meat, which sustained generations of fur traders and *voyageurs,* is still served on special occasions. Recently the University of Manitoba's football team, the Bisons, served "bisonburgers" to a visiting American team.

The Manitoba-Ontario "War." The governments of the Dominion and of Ontario had long been engaged in a dispute as to where the western boundary of Ontario should run. The Dominion government contended that it should run through Fort William (Thunder Bay); Ontario had gone to the courts to claim the southern portion of Manitoba's present eastern boundary. The courts pondered the question for years, and could have gone on pondering, except that in the disputed area there were now crews of men working on the CPR line from Lake Superior to Winnipeg. That created a difficult situation.

The contractors had forbidden the sale of liquor – which was like telling these tough hombres that they had to stop breathing. Liquor flowed and bootleggers made a mint; they got as much as fifteen dollars for a gallon of well-watered stuff that sold in Winnipeg, unwatered, for less than one dollar. "The whole region was flooded," wrote Begg. "Liquor was brought from Winnipeg concealed in oatmeal, beans, and coal oil barrels."

How could the traffic be controlled? Which province should try to control it? The one town of any size was Rat Portage (Kenora); but which province was it in? Nobody knew. But Manitoba, accepting the Dominion's boundary, set up a court at Rat Portage; and as Ontario already had a court there, the stage was set for another of our long series of comic operas.

Both provinces stationed policemen there, and Ontario's broke

123

open Manitoba's jail. The rival magistrates and police even arrested each other. And when, as it happened, the two provinces held their elections on the same day, the people of Rat Portage and district had the fun of voting in both. But the true Gilbert-and-Sullivan touch came when Ontario's Chief of Police actually arrested and held in jail Manitoba's Chief of Police. Later, in 1884, the Privy Council awarded the territory between Lake Superior and the Lake of the Woods to Ontario. But there were complications. It actually took a total of seventy-four years and forty-three Dominion-Provincial Acts and Orders-in-Council to settle the question.

The New Towns' "War." This was a battle of wits which involved trying to figure out where the main line would run. The most famous case is that of the two Grand Valley men who tried to out-smart a party of CPR officials.

Two brothers, Dougall and John McVicar, had settled in a beautiful valley some 130 miles west of Winnipeg; and when news seeped through that the main line was likely to come close and perhaps pass through the valley, settlers gravitated to it. One night there was a knock on the McVicar's door. It was General Rosser, the CPR's chief engineer, with two officials, and they were looking for a site for the first divisional point west of Winnipeg. Apparently they decided that the McVicar's 320-acre farm was just right; and after discussions that went on throughout most of the night, they agreed (according to one of several versions of the story) to pay $30,000 for it. Then they retired to sleep for the hour or two before daylight; the brothers probably just sat and stared into space. But one of them suddenly jolted the other: "Let's tell the neighbours!" They shouldn't have. The neighbours' advice was to hold out for $60,000.

When the officials awoke, the McVicars looked at Rosser, but saw only $60,000 – and asked for it. But Rosser wouldn't go for it. "Hitch up, boys," he said, and the fairy godmother vanished over the hill, leaving two saddened farmers.

The CPR men had their rig ferried across the Assiniboine, then drove west two miles. There they bought the farm of a settler named Adamson, but not for $60,000. That half-mile square, which was Adamson's farm, is today the heart of the city of Brandon. The McVicars eventually sold their holdings for $1,500.

The CPR's *"War."* That a railway was built from coast to coast before the days of modern technology seems almost a miracle. It was accomplished, to a large degree, because James J. Hill, the financial wizard, discovered a railroad-building expert, William Van Horne. Van Horne was an American who had thrown away his future, or so it seemed, to take on the job – at "some outlandish place called Winnipeg."

He arrived here on New Year's Eve, 1881, when the temperature was forty below. His reception by the newspapers was even cooler: one wrote, "The Company is wrong to hire a damned Yankee alien!" Every American was suspect – the Yankees were just waiting for the right opportunity to take over the Canadian Northwest! This hostility stopped Van Horne about as much as a fly stops a locomotive: he went right to work. And his men soon discovered that, as one said, he was not so much a man as a dynamo. He could sit up all night playing poker – he loved to "clean out the boys" – then put in a sixteen-hour day. "Sleep," he said once, "is only a habit."

He cleaned out the boys in another sense too: he got rid of the deadwood in management. He even fired General Rosser – in a violent scene in the Manitoba Club in which they both drew pistols. He soon had gangs working all over the country and, like a man driving a six-horse team, he directed and coordinated their work with uncanny efficiency. He didn't "give a continental" how railways *had* been built – he was going to try anything.

Some tasks seemed impossible. In the muskeg wilderness north of Lake Superior, the workers would lay the track – and practically see it sink into the muskeg. At the worst spot, seven sets of track were laid one on top of the other. To blast through the rocks Van Horne had dynamite factories built at three strategic locations. One particularly tough mile of track cost $700,000 and several cost half a million.

The prairies presented few obstacles, so he demanded speed. And got it: track-laying foreman Donald Grant – who incidentally was seven feet tall – simply lived to make track-laying records. His men, too, it seems, were as obsessed as he was with speed. Sometimes, to finish a stretch, they would work at night. The result was sensational: in one three-day period, they laid twenty miles of track!

The Rockies were a nightmare but there, too, the "impossible" was accomplished. And one day five years later – not ten as promised – Donald A. Smith drove that famous last spike, completing the longest railway in the world, through the world's toughest terrain! This was accomplished by Canada's four million people – one tenth of the population of the United States. Perhaps the honour of delivering the last sledge hammer blows should have gone to George Stephen. Although both men had pledged their personal fortunes – down to their gold cuff links – it was Stephen who had solved the many financial crises.

The First Train. On July 1, Dominion Day, 1886, the first transcontinental train pulled into Winnipeg from the East. The tracks were lined with wildly cheering people, the military fired a thunderous *feu de joie,* and there were banners, speeches, and various ceremonies. Then the historic train was off for Vancouver, and Winnipeg turned all its attention to three days of celebration: a regatta on the Red, horse races, lacrosse, baseball, field sports. And there was a thrilling climax: a daredevil in a balloon, soaring – like the West's aspirations – up and up and out of sight!

The CPR had "made" Winnipeg, and two weeks later, John A. – who had "made" the CPR – visited the city. It was a memorable occasion; when he spoke in the Royal Roller Skating Rink, the place was packed, and not just with Conservatives. In his opening words he showed the simple, human approach that had won him so many elections. He said, "Gentlemen, I told my friends a few years ago that at my age I could not expect to live to see the railway completed – that I would have to look down on it, from above. Some of my Liberal friends were so kind as to suggest that I might have to look up, from below. But I have disappointed both friends and foes – I am now seeing it on the horizontal."

A few days later, Sir John and Lady Macdonald were speeding West. Through the Rockies section of the line, another "Lady" was honoured: the CPR's first locomotive, the "Lady Dufferin," was put on to pull the train. And Lady Macdonald showed the derring-do that made her a fit mate for John A.; she rode part of the way in *front* of the "Lady Dufferin" – on a chair fastened above the cow-catcher.

"Big John" Norquay. Somebody described "Big John" Norquay as "three hundred pounds of fighting Conservative." Someone

else has said that "politics make strange bedfellows"; and one night, after delivering a speech in Brandon, Norquay had to share a bed with Sam Bower – who was almost as heavy. Both survived – only the bed was never the same again.

John Norquay of part-Indian ancestry, was born in the St. Andrew's settlement in 1841. The buffalo herds were not so distant in those days, and as a boy he went on many a hunt. One of his stories concerned a buffalo bull that invaded a farm herd of cows near St. Andrew's. A domestic bull objected – this was his harem! The result was a glorious bull fight, ending with the monarch of the plains tossing the lord and master of the barnyard into the river.

At age eighteen John began a three-year stint as a teacher at Parkdale. There he had two great loves. One was dancing; when he went off to a dance he always carried something on his hip – an extra pair of moccasins. He had learned from experinece that he would need them before morning. His other love was Elizabeth Setter. Elizabeth lived at High Bluff, fifty miles from Parkdale, and he wore out even more moccasins going to see her on weekends. When they were married he became a High Bluff farmer.

But John was a born leader; at age twenty-nine he ran for Manitoba's first legislature and was elected. Within a year he was a Cabinet Minister. He never lost an election, one chief reason being that, like John A., he was a born story-teller. Before starting to tell a story, he would laugh, and all three hundred pounds of him would shake. Once at an election meeting his opponent, by a trick, got the audience moving out before his turn came to speak. John began to laugh: that stopped some of them. Then his powerful voice filled the hall as he began to tell one of his famous stories. People sat down to enjoy it. He eased them into listening to his political platform – then, wrote a reporter, "Even those who came to jeer remained to cheer."

John Norquay became Premier in 1878, before the CPR was built. But when the "disallowance" question developed – should Manitoba be allowed to grant charters for branch lines connecting with American lines – friends began to fall off; the reason being that he was not pressing Ottawa as hard as they thought he should have. Pressing John A. harder would probably not have moved him from his position that the CPR must be given time to get on its feet. Cynics, of course, said that the old master-politician at Ottawa could afford to rile the West; most of the votes in the House of Commons were Eastern votes.

But Norquay did grant charters – only to have them disallowed; but he went on granting them. And he practically commuted between Winnipeg and Ottawa begging for some sort of compromise. He might as well have stayed home, which is eventually what he did. But that did not mean that he had surrendered; in fact, he now proceeded to defy Ottawa. The Manitoba government, he announced, would build a branch line itself! So one bright morning the Premier of Manitoba stuck a shovel in the ground and turned the first sod of the Red River Valley Railway. At that moment the whole cheering population would have agreed with the man reported to have exclaimed, "Big, hearty, broad-minded, eloquent, noble John Norquay!"

But idols fall. The Liberals under Tom Greenway proceeded to take advantage of a combination of local circumstances; Norquay's colleagues let him down, and he was put out of office. To add to the irony, within a few weeks Conservative Macdonald gave the new Premier, Liberal Greenway, what he had denied Conservative Norquay: an end to the "disallowance" policy.

Perhaps that's what finally broke John Norquay's heart; and his health – he died a year and a half later, aged forty-eight. But politics is a strange game: one of the wreaths at the funeral said: "John . . . in loving memory . . . Tom." Only then was it discovered that his hottest political foe, Tom Greenway, had long been his warmest personal friend.

Maybe someone farther West was listening when a lady, in a eulogy, spoke of John Norquay as a "shining peak among the little hills of men." At any rate, a shining peak in the Rockies, "Mount Norquay," was named after him.

The "Battle" of Fort Whyte. Greenway's new government decided not to go ahead with the Red River Valley Railway but to lease it to a private company. The CPR applied and was turned down: one of the chief purposes of the branch line was to provide competition for that company. In the end the government entrusted it to a subsidiary of the American railway, the Northern Pacific.

The "moment of truth" had come. To build the Red River Valley line it was necessary to cross CPR tracks; and the CPR, angry that its offer had been turned down, refused indignantly to

128

allow it. Its top brass in the West, William Van Horne and William Whyte, nearly blew their boilers; said, in effect, "Over our dead engines will they cross our tracks!" Of course, Manitobans saw this as nothing but another exercise of the monopoly they thought they had overturned; the whole province was behind its government. So the battle was joined – if the tracks were not.

The crossing was to be made at a spot six miles southwest of Winnipeg. The CPR's generals took the field. Whyte assumed command at the crucial spot (it was at once dubbed "Fort Whyte"), sat in his private car behind a live engine, and kept in touch by private telegraph line with General Van Horne at staff headquarters, the CPR office in the city. The government, with the authority of the Lieutenant Governor (none other than Dr. Schultz), asked the citizens of Winnipeg if they would like to "put the CPR in its place." Almost every man-jack in the city who did not work for the CPR volunteered, and the day the track-layers of the Red River line were to reach the CPR tracks three flatcar loads of these provincial patriots reached the battlefield – only to find that the track-layers had not. The "special task force" withdrew, but were back in two days, and this time they found themselves excluded. The CPR had built a fence around its property. And had dumped an engine in the path of the track-layers.

Then one dark night the attackers tore up enough of the CPR tracks to put in a "diamond," the necessary piece of cross-tracks, and withdrew. Exit laughing. But they left only twenty-two men on guard. General Whyte strode onstage with fifty men, drove the villains off, tore up the "diamond," and carried it in triumph back to the city. That spread the battle to the city, and to the saloons, so the Mayor called a public meeting. The net result of the meeting was that every chair was smashed.

Soon the CPR command had two hundred men on guard at Fort Whyte, with a train moving slowly up and down. General Van Horne had provided sleeping cars for his army and was even sending out hot meals. On Sunday, General Whyte's secretary brought hymn books and held a church service at the track-side. To the enemy, it must have sounded like mock-mourning for a dead cause.

Long before, of course, the case had gone to the courts, and now it was being pondered by the Supreme Court. But the battle went on. Two armies now, and two trains. Where the trains almost touched, there was a bonfire in the ditch every night, and sitting on opposite sides were men from the two armies, warming themselves, and not speaking to each other. An explosive situation – both sides had guns!

How did it end? The province won; the Supreme Court decided that the Government of Manitoba had been right in the first place. And so ended the era of railway monopoly in Manitoba, and all such railway ructions as the Battle of Fort Whyte.

The Schools Controversy. In 1870, the new Manitoba Legislature passed an Education Act which perpetuated the old "separate" system but provided all schools with public funds. There were soon far more Protestant schools than Catholic. With the coming of more and more Ontario settlers, little red Protestant school houses began to dot the landscape. The Ontarians brought with them the view of "schooling" commonly accepted back in Ontario. The lot of the teacher can be gauged by the "rules of conduct" issued to elementary teachers by a town-school principal in 1880:

> Each teacher will bring a bucket of water and a scuttle of coal for the day's session . . . will fill lamps, clean chimneys and trim wicks. Men teachers may take one evening each week for courting purposes, or two evenings if they go to church regularly. After school, teachers should spend the remaining time reading the Bible or other good books. Women teachers who marry or engage in other unseemly conduct will be dismissed. Every teacher should lay aside a goodly sum so that he will not become a burden on society. Any teacher who smokes, uses liquor, frequents pool or public halls, or gets shaved in a barber shop, will give good reason to suspect his worth, intentions, integrity, and honesty. The teacher who performs his labour faithfully and without fault for five years will be given an increase of 25 cents per week in his pay if the School Board approves.

The people living in the one relatively populated area in the province had the task of establishing a school system within a school system. In 1871, Winnipeg's citizens elected a school board of three men. They rented a log shanty between Maple Street (now Higgins Avenue) and Henry Street, and on October

31, 1871, opened Winnipeg's first public school. The teacher, for the first year, was W.F. Luxton; his salary, "to be paid when collected," $500. The next year he left and started the *Manitoba Weekly Free Press.*

It had early become apparent that the dual system could not last indefinitely. By 1885, the French-speaking Manitobans, who made up most of the Catholic population, were a small minority. By that time, too, the province's character was fast becoming that of the settlers from British Ontario; these new Manitobans were inclined to the opinion, especially observable in the United States, that democracy in education implied the separation of church and state. The result was that in 1890 the Manitoba Legislature passed an act setting up a single, tax-supported public school system.

There was trouble at once. The opponents of the act contended that it was unconstitutional, and as a test case, Dr. J.K. Barrett, a Catholic, challenged the right of the School District of Winnipeg to compel him to pay taxes for the support of its schools. The Manitoba courts found against him, the Supreme Court of Canada reversed the judgment, then the Privy Council in England reversed the decision of the Supreme Court. A similar fate was suffered in a suit brought by Anglican taxpayers.

These decisions climaxed three years of bitter conflict, intensified in the last two years by the build-up of the controversy, and the feud between the two Winnipeg newspapers, the *Free Press* and the *Tribune,* which had just begun publishing. The *Tribune* was in favour of the act, and its first edition following the flashing of the Privy Council's decision trumpeted the news (for those days) in blaring headlines. In the spirit of partisanship engendered by the controversy, and in its effort to show the *Free Press* writers how wrong they had been, it went so far as to say that "Roman Catholics have expressed satisfaction at the decision of the Privy Council."

Horse Cars vs. Electric Street Cars. Back in 1881, Bert Austin, a lad of twenty-three from Toronto, was awarded a franchise to operate a horse-car system. And on October 21, 1882, a whip cracked in the crisp morning air, a creaking horse car jolted down Main Street from the old Fort Garry gate to the City Hall, and Winnipeg's first street car system was born. But Bert began watching the experiments in other cities with electric street cars

131

and in 1891 he asked the City Councillors for permission to try them here. They were shocked. What! Live wires strung over people's heads! And live tracks that they might step on! Bert explained why their fears were groundless and they said, "Well, try it – out in the bush!"

He did, and ran a line along River Avenue from Main Street. And the experiment proved successful. Too successful: another railway syndicate persuaded the City Council to give it a franchise for an electric system.

So it now looked as if Bert Austin was really out in the bush, and up the creek, when he thought he had the inside track. But he didn't give in. He simply pointed out to the Council that he still had a horse-car franchise and he was going to keep his horse cars running. The result was that for nearly two years, 1892 to 1894, Winnipeg had both electric cars and horse cars. On the same streets: four sets of tracks, the horse cars on the two inside tracks.

How did they compare for service? The electric cars were faster, of course; they could go seven miles an hour. But sometimes their motors went dead, nearly always when it rained – there would be a short circuit; and snowstorms rendered them useless. Nothing seemed to stop the horse cars. In winter they changed from wheels to runners and the horses could generally plow through the biggest snowdrifts.

Which did people use most? Everybody took sides, became almost belligerently pro-electric or pro-horse and boycotted the other service. The feud even split families – sometimes hilariously. One story, long told by oldtimers, concerned the Sanfords. John Sanford, it seems, was pro-horse, his two maiden sisters, who worked for him in his store, pro-electric. God, they said, meant horses to run free. And one day when John unavoidably took an electric car to the store it hit a snowbank and died. He walked on to the store, opened the door and bellowed at his sisters, "Electric cars! Haw, haw, haw!" But just at that moment they heard shouting from the street and saw a horse-car horse rear up, bite the conductor, dump the car, break loose and hit out for the open prairie. The sisters gave voice to a ladylike "Haw, haw, haw!"

How did *this* comic opera battle end? First, a blow was struck for the humanitarian wing of the anti-horse car side – by a horse! Some workmen had forgotten to make a new track shock-proof and the horse either forgot to use horse-sense or decided to make the supreme sacrifice for the cause of horse-freedom. It stepped on the track and died. That, of course, didn't settle the question; hot tracks weren't enough. But a hot fire was. The horse-car barns burned down and forty-four horses died for the cause. That did it: Bert Austin had to sell out. Horsepower had won over the horse – with the help of the horse.

Norquay School and Captain Jack. In 1882, the year the first horse cars ran, Winnipeg opened its most historic school; and named it after Manitoba's most-loved native son, John Norquay. The Norquay is historic because it was built on Point Douglas, on land which had been an early Selkirk settler's farm. And it is interesting because of some of the stories told about it, like the 1890 fire.

One winter morning in 1890, when the temperature was twenty below zero, the caretaker rushed to the principal with the news that the building was on fire. Sixty-five years later, Mrs. Jean Ellis, one of the pupils at the time, recalled: "The principal quietly told each teacher at her door, and I remember Miss Maybee turning to us, her face ashen, and telling us calmly to take our things and march out without a word, and we did. Then, after the fire, a little boy in Standard III, Frank Simmonds, found the school bell in the ashes and ran home with it. He returned it with a grin in 1952 at the sixtieth anniversary of the school built in 1892."

The principal at the time of the fire was Jack Mulvey, and "Captain Jack" (he was in the militia) became a legend to his "old boys." He was "a huge man with a black moustache and a military bearing," said one of them, "and he had the best cadet corps in the city." But Captain Jack could be mock-military as a schoolmaster. "He had a great sense of humour, especially on the playground. He'd catch us fighting, we'd hear 'Halt!' and we'd freeze. 'Fall in!' and we'd line up. 'Ready, go!' and we'd run past him – run the gauntlet – because he'd have a broom in his hand and he'd swing at each of us with gusto, and usually miss!"

Oddly enough, the school's story paralleled Winnipeg's street car era in several ways. The first wooden school and the horse cars both started operating in 1882. This school and the horse car barns burned down in the early nineties. The new stone school and the electric street cars began operating in 1892, on

133

the same day. Then in 1955, the running of the last street car and the holding of the last class in the old school occurred in the same week.

Day-to-Day Life. The horse-car drivers, who received thirty dollars a month, were getting high wages for unskilled labour. Even the skilled workers in most trades, men who had served long apprenticeships, didn't get a great deal more, mainly because they were not yet organized, or their unions had not become strong. Fortunately, the cost of living was low: bread cost 2 cents, milk 5 cents, eggs 10 cents. These prices are only from a fifth to a tenth of today's, but the average worker's wages were much less than a tenth.

Health was another problem, and many a man went into heavy debt for medical bills. Ill-health was almost accepted by the more ignorant as a "visitation"; perhaps a favourite son was "meant" to die of measles or a pretty daughter lose her hair as a result of having diphtheria. Many people were gullible enough to believe in quackery, and patent medicines with outrageous claims flourished. The newspapers carried advertisements for "electric belts" and a variety of nostrums, and buying such magic cures seemed cheaper than paying doctors' bills. So the doctors were not always made use of, even though they were willing to risk their lives attending patients with deadly diseases. A Dr. O'Donnell voluntarily attended a leper in the General Hospital.

The attitude of most people towards morals was puritanical and narrow. One example – no doubt an extreme one – was that of the young lady who was fined five dollars because she had, according to her accuser, a clergyman, exposed "more than her ankle" in boarding a street car. Mixed marriages, of course, were something to be talked about in whispers. As for divorce, even to entertain the thought was wicked. For children, "right" and "wrong" were painted in black-and-white terms; they were taught that even for adults drinking, dancing, playing cards, entering a pool room, smoking, were "bad." Old-timers remember being told that if God intended man to smoke, he would have put a chimney in his head.

The church was the centre of both religious and social activities. As well as the Sunday services, there were many week-night meetings, such as the Wednesday-night prayer meeting, and fre-

134

quent revival meetings, especially when the famous evangelists, Moody and Sankey, came to the city.

The most popular evening event, one that served the double purpose of socializing and raising money, was the "box social." Each lady brought a box lunch, the boxes were auctioned off, and the successful bidders shared the lunches with the ladies who brought them. Of course, the auctioneer usually made the evening a merry one by such trickery as seeing to it that the prettiest maidens shared their lunches with the least desirable bachelors.

For children, besides Sunday school, which all children except those from "bad" homes attended regularly, there were weeknight, magic-lantern shows and concerts in which every child who could be persuaded "said a piece." Then there was the long-anticipated Christmas concert, and the annual picnic with its races for everybody; one old-timer remembers an ox-cart race. The same old-timer, incidentally, gets misty-eyed talking about the twenty-fourth of May fireworks displays put on year after year by E.L. Drewry and the "eats" provided free for every child for miles around.

The Man Who Came Home – After Seventy-Two Years. In 1897, a man of eighty-one, Colin Sinclair, came to Winnipeg and told his grandniece, Margaret Strang, the strange story of his life. Sinclair had been born at Oxford House in 1816; when he was nine, his father, the chief factor at the post, decided that he was old enough to be sent to Scotland to be educated. But his mother was so distressed at the prospect that his father put off making arrangements. That same year, however, he took Colin with him when he went to the HBC's York Factory to transact some business with the captain of a ship about to sail; and Colin begged to be allowed to go aboard to see what a ship was like.

His father took him aboard; and the lad, after seeing the sights, lay down to wait until his father had finished his business – and fell asleep. When the time came to awaken him, the captain, knowing how anxious the father was to have his son educated in Scotland, suggested that Colin should not be awakened, but left on the ship. He promised to give the boy all the care he would his own child on the voyage, and to deliver him safely to his uncle in Stromness. The father agreed.

When Colin awoke, after the ship had sailed, he was told the truth. He cried his heart out. But everybody on board was kind

135

to him and his grief lessened – and he discovered that he loved ships. And in Stromness his relatives treated him as one of their own. He went to school and did well; through the years he received letters, a batch twice a year, from his parents.

Then the time came when he had to make up his mind whether or not to return home. For whatever reason, he decided against it; perhaps it was simply that his love of ships proved too strong, for when he was eighteen he went to sea. And he remained a man of the sea all his life.

Sinclair sailed for fifty years. And it is understandable that, after the first few years, he ceased to write to his parents – his memory of them must have faded. To his mother, no doubt, his memory remained fresh; but for long years before the parents died, at Red River, they believed that he had been lost at sea.

But his early memories, although they had faded, had not died; and at the age of eighty-one – seventy-two years after the ship had carried him away – he came "home." His few remaining relatives received him as one returned from the dead, and they took him to see his mother's grave in St. John's churchyard. What his feelings were after so many years of separation can only be conjectured. But over his mother's grave he had a granite monument erected:

SACRED

To the memory of my mother
MARGARET NAHOVWAY SINCLAIR
This last token of love and affection
is erected by her wandering boy, Colin

1897

On the back of the monument is the inscription:

CAPTAIN COLIN ROBERTSON SINCLAIR
Born at Oxford House, Aug. 12, 1816
Died July 22, 1901

A Blazing Farewell to the Century. The Manitoba Hotel, at Main and Water Streets (where Schultz had guarded the government pork and beans), had been built by the Northern Pacific in 1892. The finest hotel between Montreal and Vancouver, it had housed princesses, dukes, lords, and writers like Rudyard Kipling and

Mark Twain. "Every room," as Shakespeare said about an earlier hostelry, had "blazed with lights and bray'd with minstrelsy."

But late on the night of February 8, 1899 – during Bonspiel Week – a guest smelled smoke. In half an hour, the building was an inferno, and people living within a mile or so were getting out of bed and running to see the most spectacular blaze in the city's history. The forty-five-below weather spoiled it though, and cancelled out the work of the fire-fighters: their hoses froze. About all they could do was dodge falling bricks.

A few oddities were noted by the *Tribune's* reporter. Not until "billowing clouds of black smoke surged through the hallways" did some of the guests take the fire seriously; they had just "milled around scantily clad." Some rushed back to their rooms for things. One man saved $50,000 in diamonds; another saved, he learned later, a carton of soap. And the bar-flies, watching the fire from the street, no doubt winced "to hear above the crackle of flames the popping of bottles stacked neatly in the cellar."

To us today, two items in the full story are not just oddities – they are amazing: that the origin of the fire "appeared to be over a fireplace on the fourth floor," and that "suddenly the great chimney came down in a mass of flying debris." So there were apparently open fireplaces on all seven floors – despite the fact that fire had been the great destroyer of buildings since 1812! In fact, the year the hotel was built, the burning of the Princess Opera House had threatened much of the city's business district.

But apparently people were as philosophical about the recurrence of fires as they were about the visitation of disease. And as light-hearted: a reporter quoted a man watching the flames shoot skyward from the Manitoba Hotel as saying, "At least we're seeing the old century out in a blaze of glory!"

CHAPTER 10

New Sodbusters
by the Thousands (1900-1914)

*Manitoba's great hope was people; and Wilfrid Laurier, head of
a new Liberal government at Ottawa, was determined to "fill up
the West." But would immigrants come? "Canada" meant a land
of ice and snow. They would have to be persuaded that it was
also a land of opportunity.*

Sifton Does the "Impossible." Laurier entrusted the task of
peopling the prairies to Clifford Sifton, who was both an Easterner and a Westerner. He was born in the East, grew up in the
West, went to college in the East, practised law and politics in
the West, joined Laurier's cabinet in the East and took on the
job of populating the West. Described later as a man of "chilled
steel and flawless, machine-like competence," Sifton was only in
his early thirties when he rode out of the West to meet his great
challenge. He had already won his spurs in the Manitoba political arena and Laurier gave him a free hand. He went to work.
To do the impossible, said the wiseacres. By ridiculous methods,
said practically everybody in the country.

First, by slashing red tape, he made it easy and cheap to
secure homesteads. Then he sent immigration agents, and pamph-
lets describing Canada, to the United States and Britain and
Europe. To the States! That really brought the critics buzzing
about his ears; imagine expecting Americans to leave "God's
country" for the frozen North! And for a while the young Minister was lampooned, especially when opposition newspapers reported Americans tackled by his agents as saying, "Where is this
Canada – never heard of it!"

When his agents had had time to spread the gospel – with the aid of advertisements in some seven or eight thousand papers in the United States – and millions of booklets – there were not many who had not "heard" of Canada. And Americans came; by 1914, the total was not far from a million.

Sifton's tactics in Britain were just as successful. He had his agents distribute copies of letters written by Britishers who had already become successful farmers on the prairies. He even sent some of the farmers back to their old homes to tell prospective immigrants of the new life awaiting them. He also provided expense-free trips to the prairies for British newspapermen and parliamentarians – only one of whom had a slight criticism to make. It seems that a young Welshman by the name of David Lloyd George had to request the waiter in a prairie-town hotel not to practise squirting tobacco juice into the corner cuspidor. British immigrants came too, and in vast numbers.

So did a great many peasants of Central Europe – the "men in sheepskin coats." As soon as they heard that people were leaving the United States, the fabulous "Land of Promise," for what surely must be a land of greater promise, they nearly swamped the ships. As the great proportion were looking for free land, they came to the West.

Railway Magic and the Dauphin Area. One land development of great importance came as a result of the promotional ability of two men, William Mackenzie and Donald Mann. As astute as Donald A. himself, they persuaded the Manitoba government to guarantee the construction of a much-needed railway: a hundred mile link to provide transportation for the settlements around Dauphin. Construction was not easy – incidentally, the workmen once had to be "laid off" for two days because of mosquitoes – but it was completed; and it served its purpose admirably. Also, it paid off for Mackenzie and Mann. It gave them a toe-hold in the railway "big league"; and they stretched their operations until they had a ten-thousand-mile transcontinental line, the Canadian Northern.

The Dauphin line opened up the whole of the fertile area in the northwestern part of the province. What happened in Dauphin itself reads like a fairy tale. In September, 1896, the townsite, then a wheat field, was bought. And waiting only until the crop could be harvested, the surveyors laid out the town. In October, lots were offered for sale, and by the time the railway

139

was opened for business, at the end of December, the town could boast of seventy buildings. And Dauphin was not the only "fairytale" town. During the next fifteen years there were dozens more.

The New Manitobans. Many Ukrainian families arrived before what came to be known as the Great Immigration. In 1891, peasants in a village in the Ukraine chose three of their number to journey to far-off Manitoba to spy out the land. They set out, but at the German border they were arrested; they didn't have enough money between them to get even two of them to their destination. So the one with the least money gave some of it to one of the others, and the two were allowed to go on; and they reached Manitoba. They sent back glowing reports, and a dozen more families came. Then the Educational Society of Lemberg decided that a more scientific report was necessary and it sent Professor Olesku to study this potential "promised land." The result was a book on Western Canada which painted an even rosier picture, and more families came. The professor had been astonished to find that, in only three years, one of the two original settlers had acquired a small house and had eighty dollars in the bank.

The hardships of some of the European peasant families, before they got settled, are pretty heart-rending. Rev. E.M. Hubicz tells of the experiences of two Polish families. The head of one family, who arrived in Sifton in 1898, had barely enough money to buy a team of oxen. His homestead was ten miles away, deep in the bush. He had to chop his way through, which took him a solid week. The other family, with two small children, arrived at Selkirk in 1904; they were going to settle at Winnipeg Beach where they had a relative. They had only ten cents; this they paid to be ferried across the river. Then they took to the railroad track, the mother and father carrying their children as well as their bundles. Somehow they made it; then, says Rev. Hubicz, "they sat down on their bundles and wept." They knew no one and could not speak English; and they were unable to find their relative.

Some Ukrainian immigrants settled in Winnipeg. Peter Krachuk tells of his grandparents' experiences. John Krachuk arrived ahead of his family, rented a shack to live in on Burrows Avenue, and found a pick-and-shovel job with the City Water Works Department. Digging in the winter to locate broken water-

140

mains proved an ordeal, but he worked and saved, for two long, lonely years, and sent money home. And one glorious Sunday afternoon in spring, his wife, Anna, arrived with their five children. He had rented and furnished, with things he had made or bought second-hand, a cottage with three small rooms.

But soon there were problems. Although he and Anna were somehow able to feed and clothe their family, he could not get jobs for his two eldest, Mike and Joe, aged twelve and fourteen, because they couldn't speak English. The younger ones would have to learn English too; his children were going to become something, not just live like peasants in the old land! They would have to go to school. But what kind of school? There was one nearby but he hesitated to send them there because – well, maybe the teachers didn't teach religion. Or taught a different kind of religion. And what if you had to pay?

The resolving of John's predicament, and that of thousands like him, is the story of how the Winnipeg schools – and those with large numbers of immigrant children throughout the province – accepted this great challenge; how, by trial and error, they succeeded in helping them overcome their handicaps. School people saw the problem in larger terms than just teaching foreign children to speak English. The schools would have to prepare them for a way of life drastically different from that under which their parents had grown up; and yet not alienate them, as they became more and more Canadian, from their parents, or from their cultural traditions. In this the schools succeeded admirably.

Souris's Famous Swinging Bridge. These boom years were stimulating to the imagination. Squire Sowden, a Souris pioneer, decided, chiefly for business reasons, to build a foot bridge across the river. A kind of wooden-sidewalk bridge with wire guardrails, suspended by wire cables, and anchored – like a long skipping rope – only at the extreme ends: a *swinging* bridge. Its length – 582 feet – was 132 feet longer than the famous Capilano Suspension Bridge on the West Coast.

Queer things have happened to it, or on it. It was only a month old when a strong wind flipped it completely over. Sowden added guide wires to steady it, and the town council anchored the cables to cement blocks at several places on the river banks. It still swung of course – beautifully, rhythmically – but it didn't turn over. Now that it was safe, the towners said to each other:

"We've got something! Lots of towns have delightful bridges to walk on – but not walk and bounce both!" And they vied with each other in thinking up daring ways of crossing it. One man vowed he could ride his horse over and he succeeded, although the towners decided that most of the credit should go to the horse. Then there was the delivery boy who attempted to cycle across carrying a sack of flour. The boy made it but the flour didn't.

Today, the bridge remains a source of pride to local residents, and is the town's major tourist attraction.

Hydro in Brandon – Summers Only. About the time Sowden bridged the Souris, three men in Brandon dammed the Minnedosa; and succeeded in generating power, and transmitting it nine miles along a primitive line to Brandon. By today's standards the plant's output was puny: possibly enough to operate a modern toaster for each of Brandon's then two thousand people. But at least the town could boast that it was the first in the province to use hydro-electric power; that is for the summer months. The Minnedosa was a quiet-flowing stream, but it froze solid in the winter.

A Water Transport Dream. There was one great obstacle to steamers sailing between Lake Winnipeg and Winnipeg: the rapids at St. Andrew's. Then, in 1910, the Dominion government built St. Andrew's Locks. A new navigation era was about to begin on the Red.

The news that locks were to be built had brought about a shipbuilding boom in Winnipeg. Yards sprang up along the river front; gangs of carpenters, painters, and mechanics overhauled ships and engines, built barges and tugs, and prepared the steamers for the summer haul of passengers and freight. The Winnipeg fleet included the *Winnitoba,* which could carry two thousand passengers and thirty-five carloads of freight; and the *Bonitoba* – 725 passengers and three hundred tons of freight.

At Selkirk, a fleet of twenty-seven ships had waited eagerly for the locks to open. Now the Winnipeg market would be open to them. And thousands of acres of productive land around Lake Winnipeg which could not expect railway service for years would be served by the river boats. The boats could catch up with the

142

demand for the famous Manitoba Whitefish; and lumber could be shipped to help satisfy the building boom in Winnipeg.

May 4, 1910, was the day the official ceremony of opening the locks took place. Prime Minister Laurier was there and he spoke to several thousand people. There was a sense of pride in this great engineering achievement; and Laurier reflected this spirit when he said that the word "impossible" was not to be found in the language of the Canadian West. The future this imaginative development pointed to was outlined in a 1966 issue of *Manitoba Pageant* by Hartwell Bowsfield, provincial archivist:

> St. Andrew's Locks was to be only the beginning. Already there was talk of a waterways system on the Saskatchewan to link Edmonton and Winnipeg; a steamer connection between Winnipeg and Hudson Bay; a canal system on the Winnipeg River which would allow ocean-going ships to come past Port Arthur to the prairie city in the middle of the continent. The opening of St. Andrew's Locks was but a small event compared to these dreams.

Winnipeg: Growing "To Beat Sixty." The development of Winnipeg in the early 1900's was perhaps unique among the world's cities. It was the business centre, the "neck of the bottle" through which everything had to come and go. Through the city, eastward, poured streams of wheat for the world's markets; westward poured streams of manufactured articles for the grain producers. In 1900, our old friend, Jimmy ("Steamboat") Ashdown, made history again by shipping a whole trainload of hardware – forty carloads pulled by two engines – to Edmonton and Calgary.

To handle the ever-increasing business, the Canadian Northern and the Grand Trunk expanded their yards, and the Canadian Pacific yards grew until they were the largest in the world operated by a single railway. Winnipeg lived by the coming and going of trains. The population grew from 40,000 in 1900 to 203,000 in 1913.

The marketing of grain was of ever-increasing importance, and the Grain Exchange, established in 1887, opened a futures marked in 1903. A membership, which in 1887 could be bought for $15, cost by 1906 some $2,500 (in 1928, one man paid $16,000 for a vacancy). Commercial growth was phenomenal. And in

1905 came proof that the East believed in the West: Eaton's mammoth retail store opened on Portage Avenue.

The City Council also showed its confidence in the future by building a hydro-electric system to compete with the Winnipeg Electric Company, thereby bringing the cost of electricity down from 20 cents to 3½ cents a kilowatt hour, the lowest rate on the continent. Then it tackled the water problem, and in a few years clean, soft water was flowing into the city's homes from Shoal Lake, nearly a hundred miles away. (All Winnipeg took a holiday to see it turned on.) And Mayor R.D. Waugh rescued for the city its most historic symbol of progress. Having discovered the famous old engine, the "Countess of Dufferin," dismantled and rusting away in a railway yard in British Columbia, he had it brought back, restored to its former state of grandeur and "enshrined" in front of the CPR station.

Still a Horse Age. Except for street cars and bicycles, everything moved by horses, so there were hundreds of horse "service stations" – livery stables. When Eaton's was built, there were nine of these on the south side of Portage between Main and Donald. There were also many private-company barns, blacksmith shops and harness shops (which carried everything, even straw sunbonnets to fit over the horses' ears) and curbside water-troughs. The last horse-trough, opposite the City Hall, was not removed until 1952.

The first horseless carriage to chug along Winnipeg streets was brought in by Professor Kenrick of St. John's College in 1901. It had only three wheels and the steering rod could be turned frontwards in order that the contraption could be pulled whenever it stopped chugging. The first four-wheeler, a Haynes-Apperton, was imported the next year by Donald H. Bain, and by 1905 there were twelve owners of these "benzine buggies." One day all twelve daringly set off on a safari to St. Paul, Minnesota; three of them arrived, after a week or so of varied adventure. One hazard was driving over a big bump in the road through a town, a bump built up purposely to prevent speeding. Many towns were resorting to this device – why, some of these here tourists were tearing through town at breakneck speed – maybe thirty miles an hour!

The only dependable thing about the early cars, of course, was that they could be relied on to break down or get stuck regularly.

144

Then a crowd would gather and watch the driver "get out and get under" (as a popular song put it), and the wise-guys would call helpfully: "Get a horse!" Yet despite the jeers of the non-owners – they sneered at the low-slung Hupmobile Runabout as the "Rolling Peanut" – more and more automobiles appeared in the city; by 1910 they had become a part of everyday life. The wealthy had their electrics, their steam-driven Locomobiles, their Pierce-Arrows and Cadillacs. The odd man among the "middle class" had a Model T Ford "tin lizzie," a Thomas Flyer, or a Crossley – with seat belts – or a Brush Roadster – boasting a "mother-in-law" seat in the rear. There was also a "Bush" automobile in some centres.

Sundays Were "Blue." This was a relatively religious age, so practically nothing operated on Sunday except the churches. Stores kept show-window blinds drawn. Electricity was turned off at midnight Saturday and on again at seven Sunday in time for evening church service. No street-cars ran Sunday until 1906. In that year a protest movement started, and although ministers, including Dr. C.W. Gordon (novelist "Ralph Connor"), thundered against the movement from their pulpits, it won the day. But most people, at least Protestants, still believed in a no-work-or-play "Presbyterian" Sunday, and taught their children accordingly. An old-timer remembers seeing a Catholic priest playing tennis on "the Sabbath" and wondering where he would go when he died.

This, of course, is essentially a "family" picture. But these were boom years, and with Winnipeg again bursting at the seams, life was an amalgam, not only of the old and the new, but of good and evil. James H. Gray in his book, *The Boy from Winnipeg,* tells of the economic and political scandals, of the bars and the boozing, the gambling dens, the red-light district – Annabella Street which ironically was close to the spot where the Selkirk settlers landed. The city, he says, was a "lusty, gutsy, bawdy, frontier boom-town roaring through an unequalled economic debauch."

A British-Oriented People. All Anglo-Saxons were strongly British, in the colonial sense. And their awareness of being subjects of a far-flung British Empire was no doubt intensified by a series of events. In January, 1901, there was the visit of war

145

correspondent Winston Churchill, with his dramatic stories of British heroism in the South African War (a famous Winnipeg unit was the Lord Strathcona Horse, sponsored and paid for by Lord Strathcona); a few days later a dinner for soldiers returned from South Africa (the *Free Press* reported that the ladies who waited on them had made themselves up to look "unspeakably bewitching"); ten days later the news of the death of Queen Victoria; that summer the visit of the Duke of York, who was to become King George V; in 1910, the death of King Edward VII and the accession of George V.

Newspapers. Although the Carnegie library was established in 1905, the newspapers constituted the main reading of most families. As to which paper the family read, that was usually decided by Father, who was likely to choose according to his political leanings: *Free Press* (Liberal), *Tribune* (Independent), *Telegram* (Conservative). Mother, who had no vote, read to find out if society women looked "unspeakably bewitching" in the new hobble skirts. The comics were read not only by children and the simple-minded. Still, the Katzenjammer Kids, Happy Hooligan, and Buster Brown didn't sell more papers than any feature might, except the news, as the comics do today.

Movies and Theatres. The first motion pictures in Winnipeg (Edison's kinematograph) were shown in 1898, and within a few years there were several "nickelodeons" (admission a nickel) in narrow "shooting galleries," exhibiting early jerky efforts like "The Great Train Robbery," accompanied by a banging piano. Live, professional theatre of a high quality was brought to Winnipeg by C.P. Walker.

Walker's father and grandfather were ministers, but he went "bad" – he became a theatre man in the States in the 1890's. He came to Winnipeg because he had heard that J.J. Hill had said, "Winnipeg? She'll be another Chicago!" The only theatre he could find "worth a darn" was the Winnipeg (on Notre Dame), and it was a barn of a place; but there he staged everything from Shakespeare to monkey acts. He had some odd experiences. His daughter, in her book *Curtain Time* says that once he had to reprimand the leading lady of a troupe of lady-bicyclists, who answered, with the dignity of Queen Victoria, "Mr. Walker, I shall never put my arse on a bicycle seat again."

But C.P.'s astute business sense told him that Hill was right, and if so Winnipeggers would want a theatre worthy of their "Chicago." He would build one. The gala opening of the finest theatre in Canada – the Walker (now the Odeon) occurred in 1908. On the stage, the Lieutenant Governor, the Premier, the Mayor, and "C.P." The boxes were aglitter like the Golden Horseshoe. The bill: "Madame Butterfly," new, but already a hit.

That started Winnipeg's theatre life. From September to June, Broadway and the West End sent their best: Maude Adams, with her famous appeal to the audience to "wave your handkerchief if you believe in fairies"; Mrs. Pat Campbell, smashing windows backstage but also smashing box-office records. There was opera too, light and grand, and the great singers: Chaliapin literally swaying the audience with his "Volga Boatmen"; McCormick, arriving in time to sing in church on Sunday; Melba, with her ceaseless demand for "more oxygen"; Schumann-Heink, with her even stronger demand for beer and limburger. (At one performance she suffered from stage fright – a mouse nearly ran up her voluminous skirts.)

School Days. "I went to the Somerset School," an old-timer recalls, "and I visited it recently to try to recapture some of the old atmosphere. The registers confirmed what I already knew: that attendance was pretty bad, mostly because of disease. I remember my sister coming down with whooping cough and how I whooped for joy because I didn't have to go to school for four weeks. And whooped louder when told I could go back. It was no fun playing alone.

"It's surprising there wasn't even more sickness. Homes were badly ventilated and winter clothing hadn't yet been designed for such a climate (then only Eskimos wore parkas). Once you caught something, or even broke a limb, there was a good chance you might not recover. The little girl next door to our house died on the kitchen table because the doctor setting her leg gave her too much ether.

"When I sat at a desk in my old Grade III room I 'saw' the girls around me in their middies, pleated skirts, and ribboned pigtails – so tempting to stick in ink wells – and the boys in sweaters and knickers. And my teacher, Miss Lyons, blushing charmingly when the superintendent walked in. What patience our teachers had! And their sense of humour! One April Fool's

Day, when I was in Grade V, one of the bad boys put a tack on Miss Craig's chair and she called him up, took her strap, swung it high above her head, stopped, and in a pseudo-villain voice said, 'April Fool! Go to your seat!'

"Our principal, Ralph Brown, was a gentleman, a scholar, a stern disciplinarian, and a strong believer in manly sports. He taught full-time but somehow found time to coach us, even play himself, without acting like a teacher. In fact, if two boys squared off for a scrap he'd let them go down to the basement after four and settle the question with boxing gloves. One day, looking out of his office window, he saw two boys fighting. He came out and said, 'If I see you fighting, I have to act. But the wood pile hides the view from my office.' And he turned and walked in again. In 1917, one of those lads, a soldier in the trenches, saw his old principal killed by a shell.

"The subject we liked best was military drill. If you could keep in step, you could become a cadet and get out on the play-ground – even go on route marches – in school-time; and, with broom-handles for rifles, learn to slope arms, etc. This was in preparation for the annual parade-ground display and competition put on by the city schools at Happyland, the big field south of Portage and west of Arlington. The reviewing officer: the schools' drill director, Major Billman – the very model of a modern major-general. Every school with any martial pride had a well-drilled company there. And every cadet, resplendent in his uniform, was proudly conscious of his role in this great boy-pageant, and gleefully conscious of the admiring throng of girls from his school waving the school colours on bamboo canes.

"Holidays were pretty exciting too. On Hallowe'en night, we'd gather in a mob and jam the street in front of a store yelling 'Shell out!' till the poor distracted proprietor would heave out handfuls of candies. On the twenty-fourth of May, we'd shoot off firecrackers and put explosive caps on the street-car tracks and (we imagined) blow the street car up a foot or so. After dark we'd build a huge bonfire in a vacant lot to shoot off skyrockets around, and to smoke away the billions of mosquitoes.

"But the biggest event of the year was the Industrial Exhibition at Dufferin Park, just north of the Arlington Bridge. One year, Guy Wedick of Calgary staged a 'stampede' there with real cowboys – and cowgirls. ('The husseys!' cried all the 'good' women.) But the highlight was the year a daredevil in a contrap-

148

tion called an aeroplane actually flew through the air for more than a mile. His name was Coffyn, and he died peacefully in his bed in 1962.

"Best of all was the fireworks display every night. Shooting stars, rockets streaking up to unbelievable heights, some of them bursting like shrapnel into a 'sheaf of wheat' in a myriad of colours. I can see it all now.

"But words like rocket belong to the world of fantasy. Or rather did. If some seer had told us we'd live to see on a screen in our living-rooms, a live picture of a *man* in a rocket – and later see him walking on the moon and talking to people on the earth; or that we'd see the day when rockets of another kind would be all primed to blow us off the earth – well, I should live so long!"

CHAPTER 11

Wartime: Women Win
a "Dramatic" Victory (1914-1918)

The four years of the First World War matured Canada: the country grew "from colony to nation." They suspended the growth of Manitoba by cutting off, almost completely, the inflow of capital and settlers. While most of the province's younger men were in Europe battling for justice on the world level, a group of older women at home, with the aid of socially-conscious men, battled for greater social justice. And a new Manitoba government responded by bringing in legislation that would make Manitoba a better place for "the boys" to return to.

Early in the war, the home front was marred by corruption in government: a handful of unscrupulous men were guilty of outrageous dishonesty in the construction of the Manitoba Legislative Building. The story is a sordid one.

Partisanship was rampant. At election times both party machines were guilty of corrupt practices. Yet a bi-partisan committee of the Legislature was able to agree on the construction, by Thomas Kelly & Sons, of a new Legislative Building; the cost $4,500,000. The Liberal opposition soon began to suspect "irregularities" but the money was granted. The new building, declared Conservative Premier Sir Rodmond Roblin, would be "a thing of beauty."

Then in 1915, after two years of construction, a bombshell! Headlines bigger than the war news: "Parliament Building Scandal!" Investigation had verified the Liberals' suspicions. Roblin's government resigned. He and three of his ministers were brought to trial. But the jury disagreed, and at a new trial (by which time one Minister had died) the ex-Premier and the other two Ministers were discharged, on the grounds of ill health in the case of two of the three. Kelly, the contractor, was arrested in Chicago, sent to Stony Mountain for two and a half years and ordered to repay $1,250,000. (By 1941 when the debt was "forgotten" his estate had paid $30,000.) "The scandal," says Morton, "marked the end of one era and the beginning of a new which Sir Rodmond and his party would have found uncongenial."

Women Win the Right to Vote. A few years before the war, the editor of a weekly newspaper started a women's page and invited readers to write in and tell their problems. Hundreds did; and many letters showed the tragic consequences of some of the man-made laws. One woman wrote that she and her husband had come West to get away from liquor: he was an alcoholic. The move was a great success; in a few years they owned a well-equipped farm and had a fine family. Then came the railway, a town – and a saloon. The husband slipped back into his old ways. One day when he was away on a spree, two men drove up to the farm to tell his wife they had bought the farm and everything on it – the family would have to move. She consulted a lawyer – and found she had no claim to anything.

That letter did it. In 1912, a group of Winnipeg women founded the Political Equality League. This organization, they decided, was going to be different from most suffragette groups in other countries. Years later its first president, Mrs. Lillian Baynon Thomas, explained why and how.

Most of the other groups, she said, were militant: women smashed and burned, violently attacked Prime Ministers, chained themselves to railings, turning many reasonable men against them! The Manitoba women had organized "not to fight the men opposed to 'votes for women,' but to *explain* what it meant to women and children who were in the power of weak, coarse, unfair, sick or brutal men."

And that's what they did – for three years – conscientiously and without let-up. At every gathering of any size throughout the province, there they were – the smiling suffragettes with their badges and their leaflets. Not all men smiled back. Said Mrs. Thomas, "At many a fall fair, I placed a leaflet in the eager hand of a man – only to have it stamped in the dirt or even hurled back in my face!"

Eventually they waited on Premier Roblin and suggested that

152

women ought to be allowed to run for the Legislature. He was simply amused and treated the League's spokesmen like children. (Later he said he objected to a movement supported by "women with short hair and men with long hair.") That riled them, and what they did about it was brilliant. To publicize the movement, they wrote a play, *A Mock Parliament,* caricaturing the Premier and the legislators. And Mrs. C.P. Walker not only directed them, but persuaded C.P. (perhaps after some arm twisting) to give the Walker Theatre over to them for two nights. They charged fifty cents admission and sold out both nights!

Women played all the parts; Mrs. Nellie McClung, famous author of *Sowing Seeds in Danny,* played "Premier Roblin." And the show was a smash hit. The "Members" of the "Parliament" had the audience rolling in the aisles when they passed laws wholesale, burlesquing the real legislators in Gilbert-and-Sullivan style. But the star performer was Nellie McClung. The deputation of women that had actually waited on Premier Roblin had apparently copied down the words of his reply. Now, in the show, a deputation of "men" waited on "Premier" Nellie McClung and she answered in the same words. "My dear gentlemen," she purred, "you are beautiful, cultured men, who I am sure make good homes, and you should stay there. It would be a shame for me to let you soil your hands in the dirty mess of politics." She could hardly finish for the laughter.

Later the women tackled T.C. Norris, the leader of the Opposition. He was no more receptive to their views than was Roblin, and he decided that the way to "fix" these "truants from the kitchen" was to set up an obstacle too formidable for them. Encouragingly, he said: "Produce a petition signed by forty thousand Manitobans asking for Equal Suffrage, and if and when the Liberals become the government it will be considered."

No doubt he was surprised, and maybe a little worried, when they appeared delighted at the challenge; and they went to work. City women rang doorbells; country women went from farm to farm – walked, rode buckboards, lumber wagons; one reported riding a stone boat. Mrs. Adelia Burritt, aged ninety-three, got four thousand names! The objective was topped by thousands.

Then came the Legislative Building scandal and Norris was elected to power. He was stuck with his promise. "Those women," growing more numerous every day, and joined by more and more men, kept up the pressure. Something had to give, and

153

the women never would, so Norris did: he brought in a Bill enfranchising women.

The day it was passed, exactly two years after Roblin refused the League's request, was a memorable one. The galleries of the Legislative Chambers were packed with women, and when finally the great moment came, they simply could not obey the "Silence" rule. They cheered! And broke into song – in the Legislature! Manitoba women had become the first in Canada to get the vote.

The Golden Boy. The Norris government continued its reforms. By 1918, for this and other reasons, faith in the future of the province was being restored. In that year appeared a physical symbol of that faith – the Golden Boy. Like the Legislative Building, it had had a difficult "birth." The "Spirit of Eternal Youth," as it was called by its creator, French sculptor Charles Gardet, had been cast in a French foundry. Everything in the establishment was destroyed by German artillery – except the Golden Boy. Then, like the St. Boniface Cathedral bells, it began crossing and recrossing the Atlantic; it spent two years as ballast in a troop ship before it arrived "home." And soon this colossal figure – weight, five tons; height, over thirteen feet – was atop the dome, 255 feet above the ground. (To the people watching below, the skill of contractor Floyd Buckham's men in getting it up there without "modern" equipment was probably more fascinating than the artistry of the sculptor.) By 1952, it was a "Bronze Boy": then it was given another coat of gold leaf, so that it wouldn't tarnish. Someone suggested that the man who accomplished this dizzying task should receive a Golden Boy Award.

Happenings. 1914: no thought of war. Amusements, sports, theatre; best stage show in Winnipeg, English musical-comedy company at Dominion Theatre with obscure comedian called Charlie Chaplin.

In July, everybody going off gaily to the Exhibition, or to ride an open street car to River Park, all dressed in the fashion of the time. Women wearing ground-length skirts and petticoats, and huge hats with real bird feathers – even ostrich plumes – real and artificial. Young men in square-cut suits with peg-top trousers, button-shoes (covering the ankle), two-inch high, starched

154

collars and straw "boaters"; some sported striped silk shirts. Fathers in their heavy, all-year-round blue serge suits. In August, trainloads of harvesters arriving from the East to take off the crop (at $3 for a 16-hour day).

On August 4, electrifying news: "Britain declares war on Germany." Much patriotic fervour, parading, flag-waving. Newspapers devoured for developments. Young peacetime soldiers in the 90th ("Little Black Devils"), 79th Cameron Highlanders, 34th Fort Garry Horse, straining at leash – high adventure beckoning. In October, 33,000 Canadian troops overseas. At home, high hopes – "The boys will be home by Christmas!"

1915: despite casualties, still high morale on the home front, crowds jamming the streets in front of *Free Press, Tribune, Telegram* to read war bulletins. Then one day, horror at news of poison-gas attack on Canadian troops. War work: Red Cross, Soldiers' Comforts Commission, Patriotic Fund, Victory Bonds, funds for a hospital ship, private parcels for "our boys in the trenches." Biggest wheat crop we ever had: "1915 – and next year!" Revulsion over Legislative Building Scandal.

1916: more and more families saddened as casualties mount. Excitement over "Women's Rights."

1917: increasing war-weariness. Conscription uncovers old sores. Russian Revolution weakens Allies, but entry of United states into war brings new hope. Thrills at brilliant Canadian victory at Vimy Ridge and at exploits of Manitoba's air ace, Billy Barker, V.C. Exciting event: northern dog-teams race between Winnipeg and St. Paul; longest ever staged – 522 miles.

1918: in August, Germans again approaching Paris, and using artillery firing shells seventy miles. In October and November, world-wide flu epidemic kills twenty million. (As many Canadians died of flu as were killed in the six years of the Second World War.) For seven weeks, schools and churches closed, public assemblies forbidden. War goes on, but with the aid of American reinforcements and supplies, tide reversed. At last, victory! On November 8, false report; but Manitoba (and Allied World) goes mad. On November 11 (at eleventh hour of eleventh day of eleventh month – Armistice, victory, peace! Wildest celebrations in Winnipeg's history, before or since.

CHAPTER 12

The Twenties (Whee!)
and the Thirties (Ugh!)

The dislocation of economic life caused by four years of war lasted for four years after the war. By 1925, Manitobans "never had it so good." Unfortunately, prosperity made them deaf to the ominous economic rumblings beyond their borders. In 1929, the New York stock market crashed, dragging the markets of the world down with it. The result was the cruellest depression in history.

The Winnipeg General Strike. In the spring of 1919, mothers and fathers were in the midst of reunions with their soldier-sons when suddenly Winnipeg found itself without fire protection and other services long taken for granted. Even the telegraph was silent; until the *Free Press* rigged up a wireless station on the roof – to tell the outside world that "people are not starving" – the city was cut off from the world.

This affliction, the Winnipeg General Strike, was basically the result of an unhealthy labour situation. The cost of living was sky-high – an item that had cost thirty-five cents in 1913 now cost a dollar – wages were low, and many workers, often returned soldiers, couldn't find work. And labouring men contended that some of those living in idle luxury were profiteers who had "made their pile" by supplying war materials at exorbitant prices.

Whether or not this situation by itself would have brought on a general strike, it seems clear that extremists in the labour unions played a part. Apparently they saw this as an opportune time to try out a new weapon of economic action, the general or sympathetic strike – "to put the bosses in their places." Whatever the causes, on May 15, 1919, a general strike was called.

It ended on June 21, "Black Saturday." Eight Canadian strike leaders and four "foreigners" – alleged Bolsheviks – had been arrested, and a protest demonstration was staged on Main Street. When things seemed to be getting out of hand, Mayor Charles Gray read the Riot Act from the steps of the City Hall, but his voice was swallowed up in bedlam. Main Street was simply jammed with protesters. Some of them had dumped a street car and were trying to set it afire. Others were throwing stones at the Special Constables (armed with baseball bats and revolvers) and at the North-West Mounted Police.

Shots were fired, probably by both sides. In 1969, Henry Jones, who had been one of the "Specials" remembered seeing a man pick up a brick and "he was just about to throw it when he was shot in the wrist." Jones also told of saving the life of a fellow "Special," Fred Coppins, who had won the Victoria Cross in the war. Coppins was riding ahead of him when Jones saw the mob pull him off his horse. "I had this billy here . . . and I just beat some of those guys – they would have killed him." (The billy, which had been given to him by Mayor Gray, proved useful later too: Jones gave it to his mother and she used it for forty-two years as a rolling pin.)

The climax came when the Mounties and the "Specials" charged the mob – "like Cossacks in the days of Czarist Russia," said one witness. Some of them were knocked off their horses and they became disorganized. They reformed, charged again, and this time they actually fired into the crowd. One man died instantly, another died from his wounds; and some twenty-three others were wounded (six Mounties and "Specials" were injured). This shocked the members of the Strike Committee – as it did the whole city – and within a few days they called off the strike.

The federal government had every man who could possibly be regarded as a strike leader arrested; it could do this only under an amendment to the Criminal Code – Section 98 – just passed, in a panic session, by the Canadian Parliament. After a long series of legal battles, all except two were convicted and given prison sentences of various lengths. Charges were laid against J.S. Woodsworth, who for years had been giving himself unsparingly to the uplifting of the weak and lowly. Some of the charges were farcical; one was that he had published two passages from Isaiah.

None of the charges against him were ever proceeded with – and none were ever withdrawn.

The treatment of the strike leaders left a bad taste. Writes Morton: "Thus shamefacedly closed a shameful episode; the trials and the sentences were an abuse of the processes of justice, by class fear and class rancour."

Fair-minded people had been especially outraged by the spectacle of Woodsworth, of all men, being treated like a criminal. And it surprised no one when he was elected to Parliament – re-elected over and over again. He served as a Member for twenty-one years and became known as "the conscience of the Commons." None of the other leaders "came to a bad end," as had been prophesied for them. In fact, most of them were elected to public office. Armstrong and Ivans became Members of the Manitoba Legislature. Queen sat as a Member for twenty-one years, and during this time he was elected Mayor of Winnipeg seven times. Genial Bob Russell, most warm-hearted of firebrands – but who was sent to prison for two years – was honoured, many years later, by having a school named after him.

In 1936, all the strike leaders should have got together and toasted the Members of the House of Commons of that year; it had repealed the infamous Section 98. Because of it the strike leaders had been robbed of several of their historic British rights. They had been persecuted by a law made by representatives of the Canadian people.

Jim Richardson. Perhaps no one contributed more to the recovery of the West after the war than an Easterner, James Richardson. Scion of a wealthy family, he came west in 1919 to take charge of the Winnipeg branch of the family firm. He revolutionized it, became the spokesman of the grain trade and to some extent, of the farmers. His breadth of vision was inspiring. He saw the West in real terms, not just as a great wheatland. He saw the businessman's role as that of not only making money, but of promoting a balanced development of the wealth of the country. And he set an inspiring example.

In 1925, he started Richardson Securities, now one of the largest investment firms in Canada. He had watched "bush flying" make history in the North, and in 1926 he brought the wealth of the grain trade to support the new venture and formed Western Canada Airways (the embryo Air Canada). Then, like a boy at a science fair, his attention switched from airlines to air waves, and he established Radio Station CJRC (Canadian-James-Richardson-Company), now CKRC. Then to oceanwaves: knowing that Churchill was much closer to Liverpool than was Montreal – a simple geographic fact demonstrated by the fur trade – he drew attention to it in a simple, direct way. The Hudson Bay Railway, which had been a-building – off and on – since 1884, at last, in 1929, reached Churchill. By the first direct train out of Winnipeg his firm sent one ton of Manitoba No. 1 Hard Wheat, sewn in two-pound canvas sacks, to be transported to England by the HBC's *S.S. Nascopia.*

Jim Richardson needs no monument to mark his achievements. But there is one – not just to his accomplishments, but also to his vision. In 1929, he had started to build a Winnipeg skyscraper – a breathtaking concept at the time. Then came the stock market crash. But the financial crash that autumn postponed it – for forty-one years. A magnificent, much larger Richardson Building than originally planned became a reality in time for Manitoba's Centennial.

Tom Lamb. Some years ago a businessman, flying between various points in the North, rode in seven different planes, each with a different pilot – all of whom had the same family name. They were Tom Lamb and his six sons. When, at The Pas, the businessman inquired about conservation, he was told, "See Tom Lamb." He might well have been told the same if he had inquired about commercial fishing, fur management, cattle ranching, employment of Indians on tractor trains, and, of course, bush flying. The Lamb story rivals fiction. Someone said it should be in a book; Tom's daughter has done just this, in *Dew Upon The Grass.*

Tom was born at Grand Rapids (Manitoba) in 1898, inheriting his missionary-teacher father's love of the North, and of humanity. In 1925, finding the "bush-pilot" service "spotty," he decided to learn to fly. He became, said an associate, "a pilot *par excellence,"* and it was not long before the service began to improve. Through the years he must have lost quite a lot of money – he undertook so many mercy flights. No risk was too great for him; another of his associates once remarked that, on more than one of Tom's flights, it seemed more likely that the

159

pilot, not the person he had set out to rescue, would end up dead.

With such a father, his growing sons never dreamed of becoming anything but bush flyers. And eventually there was a company, Lambair, with twenty-five pilots, six of them Lambs. Centred at The Pas, it has played a great role in opening up formerly inaccessible areas of the North.

Tom deplored the common assumption that man's natural resources were "inexhaustible," and as early as 1925 he began developing a vast muskrat reserve. An admirable conservation project, it was also a godsend to the Indians; it provided jobs for many of the Crees living in the Indian communities at The Pas and Moose Lake. He also tried for years to persuade the government to establish protective, "no-hunting" blocks for moose, deer, bear, ducks, and geese in the game area east of The Pas. And although, to Tom, the North's natural resources were "exhaustible," its possibilities were not. Why not try cattle ranching? Impossible, said his greatest admirers. His successful big "spread" showed them they were wrong.

In December, 1969, Tom Lamb's career ended; three days before the beginning of Manitoba's Centennial Year, at the age of seventy-one. The *Free Press,* after noting with satisfaction that the previous year the University of Manitoba had awarded him an Honourary Degree, voiced the regret of all who knew him, or knew of him, that, "having made such a large and rich contribution to the growth of the province during its first century, he will not be around to see the dawning of the second."

Perhaps no white man had so won the admiration and love of the Indians. Said a venerable Cree, aged eighty-eight: "He could talk Cree; he was just like one of us." And Bishop Wilkinson, conducting the service at The Pas, said "It is given to few men to reach a legendary status during their lifetime. It happened to Tom Lamb because of his great humanity."

A Viking Hockey Saga. Hockey originated in Canada, and before 1900 had developed into an almost totally different game from its chief ancestors, shinny and field hockey. By the end of the war it had become the national game, and in 1920, a hockey team from one neighbourhood in Winnipeg brought glory to the city, the province, and the country.

A few hundred Icelandic families lived in the city's West End, not far from the old Arena Rink on Bannatyne, just west of the General Hospital. In winter, the young Icelanders almost lived at the Arena. They had their own team, the Falcons, playing together year after year, and in 1920 winning the Allan Cup. That was just the right year, because for the first time, hockey had been included in the Olympic games. The Falcons were sent to Antwerp, Belgium, to represent Canada.

It was their coming, or rather their playing, that started the hockey craze in Europe. In some countries today a greater percentage of boys play hockey than in Canada. Just seeing the Canadians practise made the European players stare in wonder; made them realize that the kind of thing they had been doing and calling hockey just wasn't. And they begged to be shown how they could improve. The Falcons obligingly coached them.

The play-off games were farcical, with scores like 15-0 for Canada. What saved this first hockey Olympics from being a fiasco was the presence of a team representing the United States. There was little hockey played in the States, but the Olympic rules allowed a Canadian player born across the line, or who had become naturalized there, to play for the States. There were many such players, and as a result the American team looked almost as good as the Falcons. Without even trying, Canada and the United States sailed through to the finals.

The prospect of seeing them play each other sent the Europeans into paroxysms of delight; the game was heralded like an epic battle between the gods on Mount Olympus. And on the great night, mobs stormed the gates to get in; lords, dukes, barons jostled with "common people." Some of the nobility even disguised themselves as servants, with the hope of getting in through the kitchen. A few actually posed as hired porters to the players.

And the game? Sizzling! To the wide-eyed fans, the speed was breath-taking. Most of the spectators were for the Falcons and yelled: *"Cahnahdah! Cahnahdah!"* And Canada won, 2-0. The lads of Icelandic descent, who in their early years had had to sweep the ice at the Arena to earn ice-time to practise, were world champions!

They were acclaimed by the world, toasted in champagne on royal yachts, hailed as heroes in every city en route home. And in Winnipeg? They were welcomed with the most delirious parade since the Armistice.

161

Only later, when the city had returned to normal, did people reflect on the Falcon story – the saga of this little band of modern Vikings. Mostly second-generation Icelandic Canadians, some had fought for Canada in the war. In the world hockey-war the team had won international honours. Thus they had proven themselves worthy sons of their fathers and of their fathers' adopted land.

Wesley Park Baseball. Old-timers look back with pride at the Falcons' achievement; they look back to the amateur baseball league at Wesley Park with a nostalgic sigh and a chuckle. There was nothing like it before and there has been nothing like it since.

Pro ball, out at River Park, couldn't compete with it, partly because it was downtown (where the University of Winnipeg is now), within walking distance from work. And partly because one could "identify" with the players whereas the pros were just imports, playing in Winnipeg for pay. So the games provided a kind of home-grown, folksy excitement, especially in the play-offs – a little "World Series." There would be five or six thousand partisan fans in the stands, as wild-eyed with excitement as the fans in Yankee Stadium. What if the calibre of baseball wasn't as high as the pros served up? The competition was keener. And far more outlandish things happened – the roars of laughter could be heard in Portage.

Every game – or so it seems looking back – produced something "oddball." A visiting "barnstorming" team had a one-armed outfielder who could catch a fly and return it in practically a single motion; he also hit a two-bagger. The Granites got a new pitcher the opposing team's fans found they couldn't rattle; he acted as if he were deaf and dumb. He was. Home-run King Joe Downey ended each of his homers spectacularly: he did a complete somersault in the air at the plate. He had been a circus acrobat. Charlie Philips (weight 250 pounds), after dreaming for years of hitting a home-run, finally hit one. And it threw him into such ecstasy that he raced, yelling madly, past the two runners ahead of him on the bases, and reached home first; the opposing team got a triple play out of this weird performance. And two of the imported American umpires were a bit unorthodox. Fred Jansen, umpiring behind the plate, could throw off his mask when the ball was struck and run so fast towards first base that the fans became less interested in whether the runner was safe than whether he beat the ump. And umpire Schuster, considered hard-boiled, had a soft spot for kid pitchers trying to make good. Sometimes when he was umpiring from behind the pitcher's box he would actually coach the young hopeful (out of the side of his mouth): "Feed him a drop, kid – he'll murder your fast one!"

The Theatre's Golden Age. Today in a Winnipeg newspaper there might be one live theatre ad. In the 1920's, there would be six: for the Walker, Winnipeg, Dominion, Strand, Orpheum, and Pantages. The Greats from New York and London were still coming to the Walker; and after the war C.P. brought in something new and different – the Dumbells. They were a group of war veterans who had belonged to the Canadian Concert Parties playing to the troops behind the lines, and they were an annual sensation for several seasons.

At the Winnipeg there were Doc Howden's Permanent Players, with a reputation as the longest-playing, continuous-run, stock company in America. What enjoyment they brought their devoted followers! Talk about that certain rapport between actors and audience; here was a sort of professional "community" theatre. No housewife, once she had begun to play her own role as a part of the Tuesday or Thursday matinee, would have stayed away for anything short of a funeral.

And what idols the players became! The only native Winnipegger among them was George Secord; he stayed on in the city and went into radio. He gave an amazing demonstration of "the-show-must-go-on" spirit. Once a week for twenty-eight years he was the voice of the "Prairie Gardener" on the CBC, and the only program he missed was once when the station went off the air. The Pantages (now the Playhouse) opened in 1914. High up on the front of the building remain these words, cut in stone: "Pantages." And at one side is: "Unequalled"; on the other, "Vaudeville." Occasionally the circuit did have an "unequalled" attraction. In 1921, one could watch Jack Dempsey, heavyweight champion of the world, toy with a string of local would-be champs. Several of the many other visiting celebrities are still with us at the time of writing.

But the Pantages could not outdraw the Orpheum; since its opening in 1911, it had become an institution. Especially for

163

students: any red-blooded lad in high school or university who didn't skip classes on Friday afternoon "to attend his grand-mother's funeral" – i.e. to go to the Orpheum to lap up his week's supply of jokes – was "chicken." And any punishment was worth suffering to see and hear the Marx Brothers, Fanny Brice, Olson and Johnson, Burns and Allen, Jack Benny, Bill Robinson (later of dancing-on-the-stairs-with-Shirley-Temple fame). One year, as a publicity stunt, Robinson raced a local sprinter down Fort Street and didn't lose by much – running backwards!

A heavyweight attraction, both physically and at the box of-fice, was Sophie Tucker; she always insisted on being propelled on stage seated on the trunk of a car. Ray Reaney, spotlight man at the time, remembers getting her a car – a Maxwell. Maybe that's where Jack Benny got the idea. Powers's Elephants were not only heavyweights but hard to control: one year some of them broke loose and explored downtown Winnipeg in the dead of winter. And in 1920, the world's most famous actress played the Orpheum. Sarah Bernhardt appeared – with a wooden leg – and demanding her salary in gold coins. But not even Bernhardt could fascinate the city as Harry Houdini did. As a publicity stunt, he allowed himself to be shackled by the police, then sus-pended head-down from a cable fastened to the top of the *Free Press* building. In about a minute he was free and climbing the cable.

The death-knell of all this was "sung" by Al Jolson in 1927, when he made the first all-talking movie. About the same time, the Jack Bennys and Fanny Brices discovered that radio was a gold mine. So live theatre sickened and died and squawky talkies took over. Eventually even the Walker closed. C.P.'s daughter describes in her book her last visit with her parents to the thea-tre, now empty and still. They sat on the stage and looked out front, and remembered. She had dreaded this moment – it would be so hard on her father. She turned to him and found him smil-ing. "*Hm*," he said. Then, "Well, Mother, we brought 'em good shows."

The Walkers left and the lights dimmed and went out, as they were going out in all the playhouses of the Western World.

"Down With Conformity!" In the twenties, most Canadians lived reasonably sane lives. But life had changed, because the war had

164

smashed old patterns, had gone far towards doing away with class-consciousness, unreasoning conformity, provincialism, and inhibitions. People were conscious of a new kind of freedom.

Especially women. Now their attitude toward male chauvinism could almost be said to be that expressed in the popular song, "Anything You Can Do I Can Do Better" – or at least "Can Do." So women gloried, not only in smoking, drinking, attending dances unchaperoned, but in working at men's jobs. Determined to be hobbled no longer by strait-laced Victorian fashions, they raised their skirt hemlines from ankle to knee, bobbed their hair, used face powder, rouge and lipstick – all of which only "loose" women had done previously.

For men, particularly returned soldiers, many of the old taboos had lost their sting. Even the most strictly reared no longer considered it "bad" to smoke, drink, play pool, dance, or go to the theatre. Less fashion-conscious than women, they made few changes in their wearing apparel. Although the "sheiks" of 1921 came out with bell-bottom trousers, sometimes with a slit of coloured insert at the ankle, most men still wore plain blue serge suits and fedoras.

In winter, there was skating and hockey, and the toboggan slides on the river. Or you might go on a snowshoe tramp (there were some twenty snowshoe clubs in Winnipeg), or on a moccasin tramp, and perhaps end up at the Cabbage Patch, now the Wildwood Club. In 1922, Winnipeg had something special: a Winter Carnival on the new Legislative Building grounds. Six-foot-high ice walls half a mile long enclosed a ski slide, a lake of ice for skating, with a bandstand in the centre, and an ice palace for the "Queen of the Carnival." On a forty-below night, of course, people might prefer to stay home and match wits with the sensational new device called radio – exulting in the morning with, "I got Minneapolis!"

Winnipeg was only two-thirds its present size. There were no supermarkets. Wholesale deliveries were made to retailers by horse-drawn lorries. House-to-house deliveries by wagons with fast horses included bread and milk rigs of every description. As both lorries and wagons were replaced by sleighs in winter, the city made a point of clearing its streets only of excessive snow. There were no stop lights, and the city policemen directing the traffic at main intersections in buffalo coats and beaver hats made quite a spectacle.

165

Town Life. Life in the most remote village was becoming more and more like life in the city, but with less hurry, less tension. Saturday night was still the big night, and every town played host to the surrounding countryside. Cars – chiefly Model T's, and "Chevies," but with an occasional shiny new McLaughlin-Buick – were parked in front of the hitching posts, although there would still be some buggies and democrats. Whenever young people heard of a barn dance, even though it was fifty miles away, they would pile into their parents' open cars and set out, ready at the first sign of rain to button on the side-curtains.

Every town had its special events and special days. The event of the year was Fair Day: harness racing (with drivers from seventeen to seventy), the show ring, the exhibits, and above all, the baseball tournament. Towns a hundred miles away would send teams to compete for first prize, which might range up to five hundred dollars. Sometimes a team came "stacked"; it had imported a "ringer," a star pitcher from Winnipeg or beyond. And what a delight it was to the other teams and their supporters if a pick-up team of husky farm-boys, wielding their bats like wagon-tongues, knocked the interloper out of the box.

Tractors were just coming in, so on most farms the work was done by real horsepower – and manpower. Harvesting, with a crew of Eastern hands and high school boys, determined to prove their manhood, was sometimes a hectic race against the dangers of an early frost or hail. The farmer's wife, without electricity, worked even harder than her man did. She prepared meals without a refrigator, washed, ironed, took care of chores like cleaning the kerosene lamps, perhaps did the milking too. An exciting time for her, but oh-so-tiring. What a relief when at last she could look out and see the straw stacks burning in the moonlight, then flop by the radio – and get Minneapolis, or even KDKA!

What did Manitobans talk about? High freight rates and the tariff on farm machinery; the many medical doctors who were flouting the 1916 Prohibition Act by writing thousands of liquor presciptions – "for a bad cold" – and losing their licences to practise medicine; rum-runners smuggling liquor into the dry United States from the "wet" parts of Canada; the new bush pilots in the North, men like Stevenson or Wop May, to name only two.

The chief worry was the high cost of living. Few bothered about the international situation – the war had been won, hadn't

166

it? In the *Free Press*, J.W. Dafoe continually warned that the League of Nations must be supported, but in 1924 when wild inflation in Germany threw up an obscure Adolf Hitler, with a Charlie Chaplin moustache, few people paid any attention.

Prejudice. In 1926, Winnipeg held a contest for a design for a cenotaph to honour its war dead, and the winner was Emmanuel Hahn, an eminent Toronto sculptor. Then it was learned that Hahn had been born in Germany. He had been brought to Canada in 1892 at the age of eleven, and he was a naturalized Canadian. But he had been born in Germany.

Vehement protests came at once from the Winnipeg Board of Trade, the I.O.D.E, the Travellers' Association, and the returned soldiers' associations. And a war memorial meeting decided that Hahn should be paid the five hundred dollar first prize and that the contest should be re-opened, but confined to "persons British-born" or born in countries which had been allies of Britain during the war! Tempers ran high at the meeting; appeals to British fair play were drowned out by cries of murder.

The protesters were happy, when, in the second contest, the judges awarded the prize to a Canadian-born sculptor; although she was a woman – Elizabeth Wood of Toronto – she was Canadian-born. She was also, it turned out, the *wife* of Emmanuel Hahn! Blood pressures went up again; but the situation could be taken care of. In a democracy, if you don't like the decision arrived at by judges, you just change it. So the good citizens simply rejected the decision of the judges because "it didn't appeal to them" (the "it" was supposed to mean the design, not the decision). Mrs. Hahn got her five hundred dollars, and a runner-up, Gilbert Parfitt, was declared the winner. He filled the requirements beautifully: he was a resident of Winnipeg and he had been born in England. His creation did not bring any public complaints.

Faith, Hope – and Despair! By 1926, life was relatively prosperous and pleasant, and the popular songs – "Smiles", "It's Three O'Clock in the Morning", "Let the Rest of the World Go By" – reflected the light-heartedness of the time. This optimistic outlook was not confined to the average citizen; Margaret McWilliams, in concluding her history of Manitoba in 1927, spoke glowingly of the province's future, "a promise of better days."

Canadians shared the Great American Illusion, as it was called later, that prosperity ("Like the horseless carriage" joke) was here to stay. And Manitobans, like people all over the world, were falling for the "get-rich-quick" device of "taking a flyer" in the stock market. Some went hog-wild and took second and third mortgages on their homes. By 1929, the pace was frenzied: "Buy, buy, buy!" The coldly analytical were worried (and sneered at as Jeremiahs): could a towering, top-heavy stock market stand against the winds of a sudden loss of confidence? It fell on October 29 – CRASH! Fourteen billion dollars lost on the New York Stock Exchange! Ruin for millions – thousands in Manitoba!

"Brother, Can You Spare a Dime?" The great majority of Manitobans were not immediately affected by the crash. And newspaper stories from New York, of investors, who had flown too high, jumping out of skyscraper windows, were just "news." There were even jokes about it; for example, a hotel clerk asks: "Yes sir, you would like a room. For sleeping in or jumping out of ?"

No one in Manitoba foresaw the results to come; in fact, there were developments that did give promise of "better days." It was in the very month of the crash that the *SS Nascopia,* carrying Jim Richardson's consignment of wheat, along with furs, sailed out of Churchill. An historic voyage, heralding, so it was hoped, the long talked of cheaper water route, which, once established, would lower freight rates. Then, on July 15, 1930 – sixty years to the day from the coming into force of the Manitoba Act in 1870 – the announcement was made that the province's natural resources, which had been retained by the Dominion, would be transferred to the province. A milestone to mark Manitoba's Diamond Jubilee!

But the shock-waves from the crash had staggered the markets of the world – and turned Manitoba's dream into a nightmare. Europe stopped buying our wheat and wheat sales dropped in volume and price. By 1932, it was down to thirty-four cents a bushel. This, along with the drought, drastically reduced purchasing power, closed factories, and forced larger and larger numbers to go on relief. Thousands of men rode the steam-drawn freight

168

trains, for years on end, from coast to coast, looking for scraps of work, or holed up in the "jungles" along the river banks.

For the Winnipeg unemployed who could get on the relief rolls, the suffering was not as great; but tramping back and forth between home, such as it was, and the woodyard, to saw logs for relief coupons, did incalculable damage to the human spirit. James H. Gray, in his book *The Winter Years,* paints a graphic picture of the degradation he himself had felt. Some men, he says, cracked under the strain, and even turned to crime.

The provincial government, its own finances strained, imposed a two-per-cent tax on all wages and salaries above $480 a year, the highest tax in North America on low incomes. Many men with families worked for fifteen dollars a week, so that even though a dollar bought as much as three or four dollars does today, they had to count every penny.

In Winnipeg, there was a heartening side to the depression. Rev. Richmond Craig, of Grace Church, formed the Canadian Goodwill Industries, "turning junk that people don't need into jobs that people do need." The *Tribune,* reporting that "there are babies being born in Winnipeg whose mothers have to wrap them in newspapers," organized a Friendship League, which with service clubs and other groups collected and distributed clothing. Many such organizations were formed; the number of people who did what they could to take care of relatives and close friends will never be known.

In the country, the depression brought back the neighbourly spirit of pioneer days. But people were unable to do much for the unemployed on the move; every town at which freight trains stopped had to go through periodic invasions of rail-riders asking for food – it was hardly worthwhile asking for a job. The men on the road found the experience humiliating, especially the more sensitive among them. In an article written years later, one of them, Len Shannon, said that, for some reason, the reception he got upon calling at one house left a painful memory. A little girl answered the door, smiled sweetly, then turned and shouted to her mother inside, "It's just another bum!" He also tells of kindness shown to him on occasion. Once the engineer of a freight train not only let him ride in his nice warm cab but, noting his emaciated condition, said, "Son, my doctor says I'm always to eat my lunch, but my ulcers are bad today – d'you think you could help me out?"

169

Some of the "bums" were doctors, lawyers, engineers, former owners of businesses, skilled tradesmen, and artists who drew chalk pictures, on the walls of box-cars. Whatever they had been, misery created a bond between them; if one got sick or hurt, his pals banded together to help him, and even went hungry to feed him. But it was all a long nightmare, with, says Len, only one compensating value: it taught a fellow a new appreciation of the worthwhile things in life, like home, Christmas, clean clothes, a hot bath. Except for one class of men among them: the genuine hoboes declared that they had "never had it so good" – this was "the Big Rock Candy Mountain."

For the farmers, the depression meant poor crops at low prices, worn-out machinery, the family car in many cases stripped down and pulled by a horse. This contraption became known as the "Bennett buggy" in derision of Canada's Prime Minister, R.B. Bennett (1930-1935), whose policies, in common with those of others elsewhere, had failed to cure the depression. The old prosperity dream had faded, and no doubt many Manitobans who had once been proud to say that their grandfathers had been among the pioneers who fifty years earlier had heeded the cry, "Go West, young man!" now often wished the venturesome lads had stayed East. But things there were not much – if any – better, either.

Manitoba and World Events in the 1930's. In 1931, it was announced that the population of the province had grown to 700,000. The same year, Japan defied the League of Nations and invaded Manchuria. In 1932, Bursar J.A. Machray "embezzled" $1,700,000 from the University of Manitoba and the Anglican Church. Franklin Roosevelt, upon assuming office as the newly elected President of the United States, told the world in one of his famous radio Fireside Chats that "we have nothing to fear but fear itself." Also in 1933, the Co-operative Commonwealth Federation (C.C.F.), a new political party just founded in Alberta, invaded Manitoba; Hitler came to power in Germany. In 1935, Social Credit entered Manitoba politics, the Blue Bombers won their first Grey Cup, and Mussolini's Italy conquered Ethiopia. In 1938, Winnipeg celebrated the two-hundreth anniversary of the arrival of La Vérendrye; *"voyageurs"* in hundreds of canoes paddled from Kildonan Park to the unveiling of his monument in St. Boniface. It was the year Nazi troops suddenly occupied Austria. In March, 1939, Hitler ruthlessly seized Czechoslovakia; but Manitobans, sickened by these depredations, turned away in delighted anticipation of a great event – a highlight in the history of the province.

The Visit of the King and Queen. Until the year 1939, the twenty-fourth of May had meant simply Queen Victoria's Birthday, Firecracker Day, the holiday that signalled the beginning of summer. But on that date in 1939, came the visit to Winnipeg of King George VI, the first reigning sovereign to visit Manitoba, and Queen Elizabeth. To the thousands of children who greeted them with cheers, and even to those throughout the province who listened by radio, it was a tremendous experience. Until then the King and Queen had not been "real" people, but rather storybook figures, portraits on the classroom wall. Now, there they were, alive and charming! An experience for all to remember.

To grown-up Manitobans this was an historic moment: British Royalty riding in majestic spendour along "frontier" Main Street! To visitors from the United States, who come in their thousands, the old-world grandeur of it all was fascinating. To ex-Europeans, who had come from countries behind what was to become known as the Iron Curtain, the Royal Tour had a special, deeper meaning. Many years later, Elizabeth M. Cam, whose parents had fled from Russian pogroms in 1906, wrote of what the parade had meant to them. For years her father had been telling her of his joy of just being in Canada ("We should kiss the earth; here are we free!") and now – he could not believe it – he, who had been a peasant, was allowed to watch, from only a few yards away, the passing of the King and Queen of the British Commonwealth. He watched in awe; then, said, "Such a thing I have to see once more!" He rushed to another vantage point.

"It was then," says his daughter, "that a great feeling of identification welled within me . . . it was then that I appreciated what my father had said so often: 'In Canada we are free.' For there were no policemen . . . no motorcycle escorts . . . the King and Queen rode, in an open car – *unguarded* – through the streets!"

Perhaps to some the Royal Visit had a symbolic meaning. The depression, people believed or at least hoped, was passing, and this smiling, very human couple were symbolic of stability – of the "promise of better days" forecast ten years earlier. In that

171

sense this glowing occasion could be thought of as heralding the end of the long season of trials. Perhaps some were reminded of Shakespeare's lines:

Now is the winter of our discontent
Made glorious summer. . . .

Their "winter" *was* ended, but their "summer" was to be both glorious and tragic.

CHAPTER 13

Our Own Times

The Second World War. Manitobans of mature years remember the war vividly; to them it is not so much "history" as part of their experience. And their children have heard first-hand accounts. Highlights of that conflict should be of lasting interest to both.

When Canada declared war in September, 1939, young men all over the country flocked to join the forces. Thousands of them had never had a job, and older Canadians winced at the thought that many were now going to get their first square meal since they were children. There was much less flag-waving than in 1914; a job had to be done, that was all. And soon farm and factory were going full blast. Camp Shilo, in the Carberry hills, and Winnipeg's Minto and McGregor Armouries sprang into life; *HMCS Chippawa* and the RCAF began turning prairie lads into sailors and airmen. The names of the recruits provided striking evidence of the evolution of the Canadian nation. They were Canadians of many origins, much more so than in the First World War.

For seven months after the first German attack, there was little action, and people began to call the war a phony war – someone labelled it "the Bore War." Before it started in earnest, Manitobans were overseas. By the spring of 1940, the Princess Pat's Regiment was in England, and RCAF formations fought in the Battle of Britain. But no Canadian ground troops saw action until the end of 1941; then the news was bad. The Winnipeg Grenadiers, without any battle training, had been moved to Hong Kong. When the Japanese overran the island, the Canadians were forced to surrender – on Christmas Day. The survivors spent four difficult years in prison camps. In the spring of 1942 came the ill-fated Dieppe raid, when many of Manitoba's Cameron Highlanders were killed. But that year, RCAF bombers joined the air war over Europe, out of which came the heroic exploits of many Winnipeggers, including Andrew Mynarski, VC. In 1943, the Canadian Corps under Manitoba-born General Guy Symonds fought in Sicily and Italy. The next year, Manitobans played another part in scourging the Nazi terror. The people of one Belgian city, Bruges, showed their gratitude in a striking way. Bruges had been liberated by a Canadian force spearheaded by the 12th Manitoba Dragoons. When the citizens rebuilt a bridge partially destroyed by the Germans, they not only renamed it "Manitoba Bridge" but flanked one entrance to it with two enormous iron buffalo.

Excitement on the Home Front. There was throbbing life at home, especially in the larger centres. Streets filled with soldiers, sailors, airmen – even attractive girls in uniform; planes droned overhead; Australian and New Zealand air-trainees played soccer at Winnipeg's Osborne Stadium, with the Maoris in the New Zealand forces staging their picturesque war dances. There were Victory Bond drives and rallies and parades and "Bundles for Britain" campaigns. The most spectacular promotion scheme was "If" Day, staged by the Victory Committee. The purpose was to show realistically what might happen "if" Winnipeg were captured by the Germans. The Committee rented Nazi uniforms from Hollywood and turned a thousand Winnipeggers into a German occupation force, complete with Gestapo agents and a Gauleiter – who had to remember to look brutal. Citizens watched them goose-step, click their heels, and "Heil Hitler"; saw them "take into protective custody" the Mayor, the Premier, and the Lieutenant Governor. "If" Day got wide publicity; in fact, *Life* sent reporters and photographers and spread the story over two pages.

Bill Stephenson. Not until nearly twenty years after the war, when a book, *Room 3603,* appeared did Manitobans in general know of the amazing role played by Bill Stephenson. Of Icelandic stock, Bill was born in 1896, at Point Douglas, and went to Argyle School. In the First War he was a daredevil flyer, shooting down eighteen planes. Then, living in England between the wars, he became the amateur lightweight boxing champion of the world, a brilliant inventor, a business leader – and a multi-millionaire at the age of thirty.

When the Second War broke out, he agreed to take on, for the British Secret Service, the task of establishing a British intelligence service in the United States. And with almost no secret service experience, he performed wonders. Persuading the FBI to co-operate, he developed (wrote David Bruce, later American Ambassador to Great Britain), "the greatest intelligence organization that has ever existed." Ian Fleming, then a secret agent, later the author of the James Bond stories, says it was "the scourge of the enemy throughout the Americans." Major Donovan, the American whom Stephenson helped set up a similar organization for the American government, wrote that he "taught us all we ever knew about foreign intelligence." And a top American book reviewer declared that "the wildest writer of thrillers couldn't invent a principal character to match Stephenson."

"The Quiet Canadian," as the Americans called him, slept only four hours a night, took no pay, and laid out a million dollars of his own money. At the end of the war, he became the first foreigner to be presented with the Medal of Merit by the President of the United States. And Prime Minister Churchill, recommending him for a knighthood, wrote, to King George VI, "This one is dear to my heart." Yet perhaps Bill Stephenson's greatest reward was being allowed to be in on the Normandy invasion. He flew over the invasion coast as a rear gunner.

Events Since the War. The year 1949 marked Winnipeg's seventy-fifth anniversary as a city, and the citizens went on a rampage. There was a monster parade with floats of every description. The hit of the parade was Ken Johnston, seventy-five, riding the high-wheel bicycle on which he had become champion cyclist of Manitoba in the 1880's. Incidentally, he had also become a long-time champion usher: ever since the late eighties he had been an usher at Knox Church.

Little did the boisterous crowds know that the next spring the Red River was going to go on a rampage of its own; in fact, inflict on them the most devastating flood ever suffered by a large city in North American history. On the blackest day, May 19, the river was twenty-five miles wide. Fifteen hundred patients, some in "iron lungs," were removed from hospitals; sewers backing up and "playing giant tiddley-winks," as a reporter put it, with manhole covers, threatened epidemic. Hundreds of houses were almost submerged – one man in a canoe paddled into his own bedroom. All this, *Time* and *Life* told in story and picture; the world again "discovered" Winnipeg.

The city received generous aid from all over Canada and the United States; cities as distant as Toronto and Vancouver took thousands of Winnipeg children into their homes and their schools. A dozen years after the flood steps were finally taken to "close the barn door." The Provincial and Federal governments agreed to pay for a twenty-nine-mile-long floodway around the city. This was a gigantic undertaking: more earth was moved during its construction than for the Panama Canal.

Two Political Upsets. From 1922 to 1958, all Manitoba's governments were "Bracken" governments. The United Farmers of Manitoba (later the Liberal Progressives) won the 1922 election but had no leader. They persuaded John Bracken, who was no politician – said he had never even voted in his life – to take the post, and he became Premier. (Among the new members of the Legislature was the province's first woman Member, Mrs. Edith Rogers, a granddaughter of Sir George Simpson.) Some of the leaders in the 1919 strike had also been elected but couldn't take their seats – they were still in prison.

Bracken's Liberal Progressive government almost became a fixture in Manitoba. However, in 1943 Bracken went East – to become leader of the federal Conservatives, although his chief opposition in the Liberal Progressives had been the provincial Conservatives. At Bracken's insistence, the federal Conservatives took the name Progressive conservatives.

Bracken's right-hand man, Stuart Garson, succeeded him and followed his policies. But in 1948 he too went East – to join the federal *Liberals.* He in turn was succeeded by *his* right-hand man, Douglas Campbell, who had been a Brackenite since 1922.

A political upset took place in 1958. The Manitoba Conservatives, having left office in disgrace in 1915, (under R. P. Roblin) came back to power under his grandson, Duff Roblin. (The *Free Press* cartoonist always depicted him as a Boy Scout; an oldtimer rather appropriately dubbed him an "Horatio Alger type.")

Duff Roblin contended that the provincial services had suffered for decades; that the Bracken governments had been too concerned with reducing the provincial debt. And he quoted historian Morton's verdict on the governments of Garson and Campbell: that they had been "debt-depressive."

On the other hand, Duff's government was soon accused of being "credit-happy." Certainly taxes and the provincial debt went up – as did the quantity and quality of provincial services. Whether he was right or wrong, it would seem that he paid a price for his derring-do. People will forgive a political leader anything except levying high taxes. When in 1968, Duff, too, succumbed to the call of East, (standing unsuccessfully for the House of Commons in Wolsely constituency) the voters "remembered" – or more correctly, forgot about, his ability and substantial accomplishments.

Then, in 1969, another upset. Duff's Conservatives, now under Walter Weir, were swept out of office by the NDP, led by Ed Schreyer. So the province reached its Centennial Year under a government that was, at least to some extent, socialist. The new Premier proceeded to make history in another sense. Since 1870, Manitoba's Ministers had been overwhelmingly of Anglo-Saxon origin; in the Schreyer Cabinet all but four were of Austrian (the Premier himself), Ukrainian, Polish, Icelandic, French-Canadian and Jewish stock.

Our Hundredth – and Three Hundredth – Birthday. The great interest Manitobans showed in the 1970 celebrations was reflected by the news media, especially in their coverage of items of historical interest. To mention a few:

Dr. J.B. Tyrrell, who long ago surveyed the province's boundaries, had just retired as President of Kirkland Lake Gold Mining Company – at age ninety-five. He then took up apple-growing! John Walker, who had been a fireman on a "Countess of Dufferin" type of wood-burning locomotive, told of the screens inside the smoke-stacks "to catch the hunks of burning wood which blew all over and could set grass fires if you didn't watch out." His age – 103! Amy Louise Clemons had been chosen "Woman of the Year" by the Women's Advertising and Sales Club. Mrs. Clemons, who speaks Cree and Saulteaux, is a great-great-granddaughter of Chief Peguis, "Friend of the Selkirk settlers," whose statue stands in Kildonan Park.

Then there was the reporting, during Centennial Year, of some outstanding events. A record "Manitoba Day" trip in early May involving six large excursion boats and thirty-five buses to convey seventeen hundred people to the mouth of the historic river. The decision to erect a controversial statue to Louis Riel on the Legislative Building grounds. The *Festival du Voyageur* in St. Boniface: "a triumph of sheer fun." Lieutenant Governor Bowles reminding an audience that a great many different ensigns have flown over Manitoba's territory or parts of it: Captain Button's British flag, Jens Munck's Danish flag, Vérendrye's French flag, the HBC flag, Thomas Spence's "Republic of Manitobah" flag, Riel's flag (with *fleur-de-lys* and shamrock), Schultz's "Canada" flag, the Union Jack, the Canadian Ensign, the present Canadian flag and Manitoba's new provincial flag. The meeting at Lower Fort Garry of Prime Minister Trudeau and Cabinet: the first federal Cabinet meeting ever held outside Ottawa. From Winnipeg to the Lower Fort they travelled in an antique railway coach pulled by "Old No. 3," believed to be the oldest steam locomotive in operating condition in Canada.

And the news emanating from the Hudson's Bay Company; it had deeded York Factory to the Canadian government to restore and preserve as a national historical site: "Our first habitation saved for our children." A replica of the *Nonsuch* would embark on a transported "voyage" to Winnipeg: "When Manitoba landlubbers spot the three-hundred-year-old ketch 'sailing' across the prairies, they'll know it's for real." The moving of the HBC head office from overseas to Winnipeg: "The Company is coming home."

The highlight of the Centennial was the Royal Visit of Queen Elizabeth, the Duke of Edinburgh, the Prince of Wales, and Princess Anne. The great historic event was the symbolic ceremony at Lower Fort Garry which brought Manitoba's three-hundred-year history full circle. Queen Elizabeth, heir to King Charles II's realms, accepted from the heirs of the "Governor and Company of Adventurers" the tribute decreed three centuries ago: "Two Elkes and two Black Beavers."

Having touched on the high spots – and some of the low spots – of our story, how should we now feel toward our province? Without being melodramatic or superficially sentimental, without indulging in flag-waving, we might echo the thoughts expressed by Gwen Pharis about Canada:

My roots are in this soil,
Whatever good or bad, what vain hope or
    mighty triumph lies in you,
That good or bad, that destiny is in me.
Where you have failed, the fault is on my head.
Where you are ignorant or blind or cruel,
    I made you so.
In all your folly and your strength, I share,
And all your beauty is my heritage.